# Egypt
## Red Sea Coast

Front cover: sergeant
major fish in Gota
Abu Ramada

Right: the Red
Sea's reefs are a
diver's delight

D0566668

# TOP 10 ATTRACTIONS

**St Catherine's Monastery** • This 6th-century monastery is at the foot of Mount Sinai, on the site where Moses saw the burning bush *(page 35)*

**Desert safaris** •
Take an excursion into Bedouin territory via 4x4, quad bike or even on a camel *(page 89)*

**Suez Canal** • See convoys of huge ships pass through one of the world's greatest engineering feats *(page 57)*

**Jazurat Fer'un** • A beautiful castle set on a small island in the Gulf of Aqaba *(page 45)*

**Red Sea Reefs** • Dive or snorkel amongst the spectacular coral and abundant marine life *(page 85)*

**Mount Sinai** • Trekking up to watch the sunrise from the summit can be a truly spiritual experience *(page 37)*

**Mons Claudianus** • There is still lots to see at this abandoned Roman quarry *(page 72)*

**Al Qasir** • A fascinating town with an ancient harbour and remarkable trading history *(page 73)*

**Ras Muhammad National Park** • The ecosystem is in pristine condition on both land and sea *(page 31)*

**Sarabet Al Khadem** • This ancient Egyptian temple with its carvings and hieroglyphics is unique in Sinai *(page 50)*

# A PERFECT DAY

### 7.00am Breakfast

Top up your energy levels with a filling breakfast from your hotel's buffet – there's always plenty of healthy fruit and salads.

### 11.30am Coastal walk

Get dropped off at the popular Mashraba area of Dahab and check out the ancient ruins of Al Mashraba Hill – a coastal settlement dating back more than 2,000 years. Walk along the Asilah seafront with its local stalls and bars towards the Masbat part of Dahab.

### 8.00am Dive dive dive

Morning scuba dives or snorkelling trips start quite early. A visit to a dive site by boat is usually part of a full day two-dive package, but there are always plenty of single dives and snorkelling opportunities direct from the quiet beaches, such as Shark's Bay. Morning dives are best for good visibility and calm water, before the wind gets up in the afternoon.

### 10.00am Desert scenery

After a shower, take a well-deserved coffee break overlooking the sea at Umbi Diving Village in Shark's Bay, before hiring a taxi and heading north through spectacular desert scenery to the laid-back resort of Dahab.

### 12.30pm Lunchtime

Drop in for a casual seafood lunch at the peaceful Arisha thatched beach restaurant beside the Coral Beach Hotel, with wonderful views across the still waters of the Gulf of Aqaba to Saudi Arabia.

# IN SHARM EL SHEIKH

### 4.00pm Shopping and sunset

By the time you arrive, the shops will just be opening again after the midday break. Search for souvenirs such as spices, gold, perfumes and cotton clothing in the narrow back streets. Towards sunset head along the beach and climb up to the cliff-top path, walking around the Ras 'Om Sid headland to the Sadiki Cafe for tremendous coastal views.

### 10.00pm Night owls

Take your choice from the numerous bars and clubs, many with live music and stay out for as long as you like until the early hours at Pacha Club or Little Buddha Sushi Bar and Lounge.

### 6.30pm Relaxation

Grab a taxi to Naama Bay which is still fairly quiet in the early evening. Relax with a cold drink and fabulous views across Naama Bay and along the coast from the terraced setting of Zizi Panorama.

### 2.30pm Old Sharm

Transfer back to Sharm El Sheikh, but this time continue past the main resort areas and through the centre to the local traditional area of Old Sharm.

### 8.00pm Fine dining

Reserve a table indoors or outside on the terrace at Abou el-Sid restaurant, above the Hard Rock Cafe in Naama Bay. Quality Egyptian and Middle Eastern cuisine in an atmospheric eastern setting.

# CONTENTS

8

74

26

# INTRODUCTION

The Red Sea is a narrow body of water over 2,000km (1,200 miles) in length that connects the Indian Ocean with the Mediterranean. Along its length are some of the most pristine coral reefs and varied marine life to be found anywhere on earth – just waiting to be discovered. Egypt has over 1,700km (1,000 miles) of Red Sea coastline, including the Sinai Peninsula, which is bordered on the east by the Gulf of Aqaba and on the west by the Gulf of Suez. The local population is concentrated along the coast, and the main centres of tourist activity are Sharm El Sheikh in the south of the Sinai Peninsula and Hurghadah on the northern part of Egypt's eastern coast. Towards the border with Sudan in the south the coastline is only very sparsely populated.

## Red Sea Reality

The level of tourist development along Egypt's Red Sea coast is remarkable, since just 30 years ago special permission was required to visit the area, and the Sinai Peninsula was still under Israeli control. But in the early 1980s the seed of an Israeli idea to make the Gulf of Aqaba a holiday retreat was brought to fruition by the Egyptians. Simple diving resorts were initially developed, and proved so popular that the Egyptian Tourist Authority – so good at promoting its ancient culture – quickly turned the area into a world-class destination.

Despite the waterway's continuing role as an important trading route for ships passing through the Suez Canal, the region is now extremely well set up to cater for holiday-makers, and the many resorts offer all the facilities a modern tourist could wish for. A typical day could include a

Old sailing ship leaving Sharm El Sheikh harbour

tranquil scuba-dive on a beautiful coral reef, an adventurous 4x4 safari into the desert wilderness and an exhilarating windsurfing lesson on the turquoise seas, all topped off by dancing the night away in a beachside club. If that all sounds a little too much like hard work, you could just order another drink by the poolside and spend the whole day lying in the almost continuous sunshine.

The most pleasant months to visit are generally spring (March–May) and autumn (September–November), when most days and nights are warm. The summer months (June–August) can be extremely hot – up to 42°C (107°F), whereas the winter months (December–February) have sunny days, with temperatures up to 20°C (68°F), but cool evenings, especially in the desert or at altitude. The Red Sea is the warmest sea in the world, with temperatures ranging from 20°C (68°F) in winter to 28°C (82°F) in summer.

Idyllic Shagra Village resort in southern Egypt

## Bedouin Traditions

Whilst many visitors are happy to swim, dive and snorkel in the warm waters, what they see along the coast is just a taster for what lies inland. Strong tribal links still connect the people of Sinai, and away from the coast the land has hardly changed since Moses and his followers wandered through. Some Bedouin people still follow a traditional lifestyle, travelling through the scorched *wadis* from one

Traditional Bedouin headgear

oasis to another with a few goats and camels. You can catch a glimpse of their lives on a short desert tour from the coast, or join them on safari for a few days. They still follow the routes used by ancient traders bringing goods to and from the Nile Valley or by religious pilgrims passing through the difficult desert landscapes to important religious sites, such as the monasteries of St Catherine, St Paul and St Anthony.

Whilst most local workers in the resorts have a very Western attitude and lifestyle, many are still tied to their heritage. Family, tribal and religious bonds remain strong, and children especially receive a warm welcome from all Egyptians. A tribal wedding is a time for great celebration and an opportunity for friends and family to meet up. But long gone are the days of travelling by camel, as today's guests arrive in remote villages in the very latest air-conditioned luxury cars. Even so, annual camel races are still an important event, as all Bedouin pride themselves on the quality and fitness of their camels.

## Underwater Paradise

The Red Sea's marine life is rated by experts as some of the best in the world. The nutrient-rich waters of this almost enclosed sea produce the most wonderful coral gardens and reef walls, protecting countless colourful reef fish. These smaller fish in turn attract larger predators such as rays, sharks and sailfish. There are around 200 types of coral in the Red Sea, and over 1,000 species of fish. Marine national parks and protectorates provide habitats for many rare species, including turtles and dugong.

As beautiful as the coral outcrops might appear, they are also dangerous, as witnessed by the many shipwrecks dotted along the coast. Egypt's sunken wrecks are acknowledged to be some of the most interesting dives in the world, and if you are not qualified already there are plenty of opportunities to learn one of the fastest-growing adventure sports in

### The 'Red' Sea

It is still uncertain where the name 'Red Sea' actually comes from. Some say that it is from early sailors describing the colour of the surrounding mountains, but it is more probably from a strange phenomenon that still occurs today. In certain conditions, there is a cyanobacterial blooming of the algae 'Trichodesmium Erythraeum'. When this blue-green algae dies, it muddies the normally clear waters with a cloudy reddish liquid, which can stretch over hundreds of square kilometres, making the sea water appear to be a soapy orange or red colour.

A similar bacterium causes the reddish-purple deposits often seen near the geysers and hot springs of the Red Sea coast. The area's geothermal activity is due to the fact that the continents of Africa and Asia are slowly pulling away from each other. Part of the Great Rift Valley, the Red Sea is actually widening at a rate of almost 2cm (¾in) per year – about the same as a growing fingernail.

Colourful soft coral attracts plenty of fish

the world. If diving doesn't appeal, then you can have just as much fun snorkelling along the reefs and inlets or taking a submarine ride through the depths.

But not all of the action is underwater. The natural windy conditions are perfect for wind- and kitesurfing, sailing and yachting up to world-class standards. And of course there are always plenty of other activities on offer, such as water-skiing, towed banana rides and parasailing.

## Modern Expansion

There are resorts along the coast pitched at every kind of holiday – child-friendly, sporting-centred, spa retreat – so there's no reason to end up somewhere that does not fit your exact requirements. The past five years have seen tremendous growth in the top end of the market, with luxury-hotel owners and operators opening world-class resorts almost weekly. And for those concerned about the effect that all these developments

**Nile Valley workers**

The massive rise in tourists coming here has outgrown the numbers of local people available to staff the many hotels, restaurants and shops. Many additional workers have come here from the Nile Valley, especially Luxor, due to its proximity and existing tradition of working with tourists.

are having on the environment, there are also plenty of eco-friendly resorts, where sustainability is the priority.

The main tourist centres of Sharm El Sheikh and Hurghadah are both quite different. Sharm El Sheikh is a collection of neighbouring bays, each with its own shops, bars, restaurants and activities. Hurghadah is much more open to the sea, with a wonderful seafront promenade linking all the resorts and hotels. Small areas of old Hurghadah such as the fishing harbour and market give a flavour of the 'real Egypt', which is somewhat missing in Sharm El Sheikh.

Those seeking a more peaceful retreat needn't venture far. North of Sharm's centre is smaller Shark's Bay, and beyond that the more relaxed atmosphere of the Gulf of Aqaba coast – ideal for those wanting to drop out, if only for a few days. South of Hurghadah there are many smaller resorts on the long stretches of golden sand, where the pace of life is much slower.

It should be possible to visit some of Egypt's famous ancient sites, such as the Valley of the Kings at Luxor (Al Uqsur) or the pyramids at Giza, on one- or two-day excursions.

# A BRIEF HISTORY

From ancient times to the present day, the Red Sea has acted as a highway for trade. Early activity along the sea's coast is closely associated with the pharaonic civilisations of the Nile Valley. The Red Sea was often the ancient Egyptians' major trading link with Arabia, Persia, Asia and East Africa.

Around 3000BC mines in the Sinai Peninsula were producing precious stones and the raw materials for making metals. Remains of mining operations around the temple at Sarabet Al Khadem *(see page 50)* indicate that turquoise and copper ores were obtained along the western side of the Sinai. From inscriptions along the Nile it seems that the early pharaohs had to defeat prehistoric tribes in the Sinai in order to establish these mines. Little is known about who these locals were, and the

Prehistoric Nawamis tombs in the Sinai

Queen Hatshepsut's soldiers on an expedition to Punt, 1482BC

only tangible link to this period are ancient stone tombs called Nawamis. Found only in the Sinai, the most accessible ones lie near the road up to St Catherine's Monastery (Dayr Sant Katrin), not far from Ain Khodrah *(see page 44)*. Funerary offerings unearthed inside, including shell beads, flint tools and tiny pots, have been dated between 4000 and 3150BC. The doors to the tombs face west, towards the sunset – the direction of death and the afterlife for ancient Egyptians.

## Visiting the Land of Punt

As well as metals and precious stones, the Egyptians also used a wide variety of exotic aromatic substances such as incense and myrrh, which could only be obtained through trade. Incense was burnt by priests in temple rituals to the gods, bringing prosperity to the land; myrrh was used in the complicated process of mummifying dead bodies. Hieroglyphic texts dating from 1458BC on the walls of the funerary temple of Queen Hatshepsut at Luxor suggest that these substances were obtained from the 'Land of Punt'. A picture in the temple shows a large ship being loaded with incense bushes, spices, precious woods and other valuable commodities. We know that the ship is on the Red Sea (rather than the River Nile) because the fish swimming in the water beneath it are shown in such detail that they have been identified as saltwater species.

Even though 'Punt' is referred to continually from 2500BC to 1000BC, this was probably not a single location, but simply places where these aromatics were found at a particular time, corresponding to modern Sudan, Eritrea, Yemen and Somalia. The discovery of ropes and wooden boxes dating from 1900BC at the ancient port of Marsa Gawasis near modern Safajah *(see page 71)* suggests that it formed an important part of this trade route. This sea trade ended around 1000BC, possibly due to the increase in overland trade through Arabia to Petra, along what is known as the Incense Road.

## Sinai – A Military Thoroughfare

The wilderness of the Sinai is one of the most strategically important locations on earth, since it forms a link between Africa and Asia. Under the great military pharaohs such as Tutmosis III and Rameses II the ancient Egyptians attacked their eastern Mediterranean enemies through the Sinai. In the other direction came the armies of Assyria, Persia, Greece, Rome and early Muslim invaders from Arabia.

After the building of the Suez Canal the region became even more important, with the Sinai acting as a 'buffer zone' between east and west. The Sinai was the focus of the first Arab-Israeli War in 1948, when Egypt and its Arab neighbours fought the new state of Israel. Still within recent memory are conflicts such as the Suez Crisis of 1956 and the Arab-Israeli wars of 1967 and 1973.

## The First Canal

By whichever route the imported goods arrived, there was certainly enough trade to warrant the building of an ambitious east–west canal linking the Suez area to the Nile near Memphis. In ancient times the Red Sea coast stretched further north into the Bitter Lakes or even to Lake Timsah, near present-day Ismailia. A small canal is said to have been constructed during the 18th dynasty, around 1850BC, and this was enlarged by Rameses II about 600 years later. Ships from the Red Sea could now sail – albeit indirectly – to the Mediterranean via the Nile.

The waterway later fell into disrepair, but in the 5th century BC, after the Persians had conquered Egypt, their king Darius I ordered that the east–west canal be cleared and rebuilt so that he could sail his ships straight from the Persian Gulf right into the heart of Egypt.

## Greeks and Romans

Greek influence in the region began in 332BC, when the army of Alexander the Great marched through the Sinai to seize Egypt. He built a new capital at Alexandria, on the coast of the Mediterranean, which grew rapidly. The Egypt of the Ptolemies, the rulers who followed Alexander, was firmly Mediterranean in outlook and the status of the Red Sea ports fell. With the death of Cleopatra in 30BC, Egypt came under Roman rule. The Romans returned the capital to the Cairo area, and the Red Sea became important once again. The fortunes of the Red Sea ports were firmly linked to the riches of the Nile Valley. But maintaining these coastal communities was always difficult due to the lack of water, harsh climatic conditions and problematic winds.

Most of our information about the coastline of the Egyptian Red Sea in the 1st century AD comes from the writings of Pliny the Elder (AD23–79). He described the great wealth of goods such as spices, silk and incense arriving via the 'Mare Erythraeum' (Red Sea, the first use of this name) and then transported down the River Nile. At around the same time a nautical handbook written in Greek, the *Periplus of the Erythraean Sea*, appeared. It describes the sailing routes and maritime trade of the Red Sea, Arabian Sea and the eastern Indian coast, underlining the commercial importance of the Red Sea at the time. Some of the ports and harbours mentioned in the Periplus can be identified today, including Myos

Alexander the Great, who seized Egypt in 332BC

Hormos (modern Al Qasir, *see page 73*). The other major Red Sea ports of Greek and Roman times were Arsinoe, Clysma and Berenice. Goods were transported overland from these ports to the River Nile and the Mediterranean. Although the distance was less from the northern ports, the southern ones had a big advantage – they were protected from unfavourable winds. The direction of the prevailing winds means that it is easy to sail south out of the Red Sea into the Indian Ocean, but extremely difficult to sail back north. Goods carried in large trading ships were transferred into smaller dhows for the northward journey at ports like Jeddah (in what is now Saudi Arabia) and Suakin (in Sudan); otherwise, travelling north up the Red Sea required an arduous period of rowing against the wind. The Greeks and Romans understood this, which is why they focused more on Myos Hormos and Berenice, the most southerly ports under their control. From here they carried the goods overland through the mountains to the Nile.

**St Catherine**

The trade continued into the Byzantine period. In the middle of the 6th century, the emperor Justinian built a monastery on the supposed site of Moses' encounter with the burning bush, on the Sinai Peninsula. It was named after Catherine, a 3rd-century saint from Alexandria.

## The Arrival of Islam

In 639, seven years of the death of the prophet Mohammed, Islam was brought to Egypt when Arab invaders crossed the Sinai and established themselves in Fustat. Successive Islamic dynasties eventually created the great city of Cairo. The Red Sea and the Sinai remained important stops on pilgrimages to the Holy Cities.

Islamic lattice-work

Crusader threats to Egypt were crushed when Saladin, the Sultan of Egypt, and his army crossed the Sinai in 1182 to fight the Crusaders. The sultan's great legacy is Jazurat Fer'un – the island castle just south of Taba. In the 13th century, Marco Polo glamorised the overland trade from Asia to Europe along the 'Silk Road', but even he noted that much of the trade also went by sea via the Indian Ocean and Red Sea.

From 1250, Egypt experienced nearly three centuries of chaotic Mameluke rule, which gave way to the might of the Ottoman Empire in 1517. The Red Sea once again became a busy trade route under Ottoman protection, which helped to spread a little-known commodity used primarily in Yemen and Ethiopia – coffee. The oldest known reference to coffee as a traded commodity is in a letter written in 1497 found at the port of At Tur in Sinai. A miniature painting shows the Ottoman Sultan Suleiman the Magnificent drinking coffee in 1522, and shortly afterwards Venetian traders introduced the beverage into Europe, where the British became the first to adopt the idea of commercial coffee houses in around 1650.

Cutting through the final section of the Suez Canal, 1869

Yemen had a world monopoly on coffee production, but this ended in the 17th century when the Dutch smuggled out some live coffee bushes and replanted them in Java.

European nations had long wanted direct access to the markets of Asia, without having to deal with Ottoman interference. There were practical problems too. The Portuguese coffee traders of the 16th century faced the same wind-direction challenges as the early sailors. In 1541 navigator João de Castro reported that it took 66 days of almost constant rowing to get up the Red Sea to Suez, but the return journey was only 25 days, sailing all the way.

## The Suez Canal

In the late 16th century, Portuguese explorers pioneered a new sea route to Asia around southern Africa, and for about 300 years the Red Sea became a minor backwater, as all trade bypassed the area. But in 1869 the region's fortunes revived with the opening of the Suez Canal – the greatest engineering project of the time – by Belgian engineer Ferdinand de Lesseps. The Red Sea was now linked directly to the Mediterranean, greatly reducing the sailing time between Europe and eastern Asia. Although Egypt was still nominally part of the Ottoman Empire until World War I, Britain controlled both the canal and Egyptian affairs, a situation that provoked internal unrest for decades.

Britain granted Egypt independence in 1922, but continued to dominate the country. The immediate post-War World II period was decisive. In 1952 Egypt overthrew its ruler, King Farouk, and freed itself of British control, but it was soon again in conflict with both Britain and Israel in the Suez Crisis *(see below)*.

In 1948, after the state of Israel was established, Egypt had taken part in the first Arab-Israeli War. In June 1967, the Israelis again attacked Egypt in the Six Day War, and held the Sinai Peninsula up to the edge of the canal. Heavy bom-

## The Suez Crisis

While Britain defended the Suez Canal during both world wars it imposed strict controls on Egypt. For Egyptians, foreign possession of the canal came to represent the major reason for the anti-imperialist struggle. Although independence was achieved in 1952, it was not until 1954 that President Nasser forced the withdrawal of British troops occupying the Canal Zone. Egypt still received only a tiny portion of the canal's revenue from Britain. Seeking to finance the Aswan High Dam and having been refused money by the United States, Nasser nationalised the canal. Together with the French and Israelis, Britain responded by invading the Canal Zone, in what became known as the Suez Crisis. Only the intervention of the two superpowers resolved the situation, after which Egypt started a long and dependent relationship with the Soviet Union.

bardment during the War of Attrition, which followed this Israeli conquest, shattered the canal cities and made refugees of their 500,000 inhabitants. The waterway was closed to traffic until the successful Egyptian counterattack in the Yom Kippur War of October 1973, under President Anwar Sadat. Reopened in 1975, the canal has since been widened and deepened several times. The Camp David Peace Agreement of 1979 gave Egypt permanent control over the Sinai. Sadat was assassinated in 1981 and replaced by Hosni Mubarak.

Egyptian hotels were built on Sinai to cater for adventurous divers keen to get a glimpse of newly opened marine areas, including Ras Muhammad, which became the first national park. Egypt's massive tourist industry – hitherto focused on the wonders of ancient Egypt – now had a new destination to promote.

Tourist numbers grew rapidly in the first years of the 21st century. Sinai's future was clouded by the tragic terrorist bombings in Taba, Sharm El Sheikh and Dahab between 2004 and 2006, but despite this, visitor numbers have continued to rise year on year. As part of the 'Arab Spring' revolutions sweeping across the Middle East, Hosni Mubarak was forced to resign in February 2011 following mass demonstrations in Cairo and other major cities. Mubarak was subsequently arrested on charges of conspiring to kill protesters, and set to stand trial. A temporary government supported by the army is to oversee new democratic elections.

**Men celebrate Mubarak's step down in Tahrir Square**

# Historical Landmarks

**c.3000BC** Sinai used as a source of precious stones and metal ores by Nile Valley dynasties.

**c.1500BC** Queen Hatshepsut's trade mission along the Red Sea to bring back incense, spices and precious woods.

**332BC** Alexander the Great marches through the Sinai and seizes Egypt. Start of Ptolemaic period.

**30BC** Egypt becomes a province of Rome.

**c.AD550** St Catherine's Monastery constructed under the Byzantine emperor Justinian.

**639** Islam brought to Egypt as Arab invaders cross the Sinai and establish themselves in Cairo.

**1182** Saladin, Sultan of Egypt, and his army cross the Sinai to fight against the Crusaders.

**1517** Ottoman Turks invade Egypt. The Red Sea becomes a busy internal trade route under their protection.

**1869** The Suez Canal opens.

**1922** Egypt is granted independence.

**1948** Egypt is involved in the first Arab-Israeli War after the establishment of the state of Israel.

**1956** The Suez Crisis follows President Nasser's nationalisation of the Suez Canal. Britain, France and Israel occupy the Canal Zone and the Sinai, but withdraw after international condemnation.

**1967** Six Day War. Israel attacks Egypt and occupies the Sinai.

**1973** 6 October War (Yom Kippur War). Egypt retaliates against Israeli occupation and regains the East Bank of the Suez Canal.

**1979** Camp David Peace Agreement gives Egypt control over the Sinai; Israel withdraws troops.

**1983** Ras Muhammad declared a protected area.

**2004–6** Terrorist bombs kill over 100 people in Taba, Sharm El Sheikh and Dahab.

**2011** Hosni Mubarak resigns after 30 years as president following nationwide uprisings. He is arrested on charges of trying to kill protesters.

# WHERE TO GO

Egypt's Red Sea coastline is over 1,700km (1,000 miles) long, requiring plenty of time and effort to see it all, especially the remote southern area near the border with Sudan. The most prominent geographical feature is the triangular Sinai Peninsula in the north, which splits the Gulf of Suez from the Gulf of Aqaba. Most visitors stay within a relatively small area of their resort, making excursions out to the spectacular coral reefs or inland to the famous historical and biblical sites that border this ancient trading waterway.

## SHARM EL SHEIKH AND SOUTH SINAI

Most of what we see along this part of the coast has been built since Israel handed the Sinai back to Egypt in 1979. What began as basic resorts for holidaying Israeli soldiers has developed into a huge international tourist playground. The main resort in South Sinai is Sharm El Sheikh, meaning 'coastal inlet of the tribal chief', which covers a long stretch of coastline with many smaller bays and centres. Most visitors to Sinai will arrive at the international airport, just northeast of the resort. The choice of dive sites in the area is endless, and despite headlines of shark attacks as recent as December 2010, such incidents are extremely rare.

### Sharm El Sheikh

The region of **Sharm El Sheikh** (Sharm Ash Shaikh) covers everything from Sharm Al Maya, Old Sharm, Ras 'Om Sid and Hadaba in the southwest around to Naama Bay, Coral Bay, Shark's Bay, Ras Nasrani and past the airport to Nabeq in the

Pilgrim on Mount Sinai

northeast. At first it can be quite confusing to understand the layout of Egypt's most popular tourist destination. Distances between the resorts make walking difficult – especially in the heat – but there are many taxis and minibuses running along the main highway, **Peace Road**, which links all the bays. 'Sharm' promotes itself as 'Peace City' – a venue for international peace conferences, which are held in the large resort hotels.

At the western end is the main port of **Sharm Al Maya**, beyond which the road runs west towards Ras Muhammed, Suez and Cairo. Hundreds of dive boats are moored in the harbour, which is also the departure point for the ferry to Hughadah (Al Ghardaqah). Inland is **Old Sharm** – as authentic a piece of Egypt as you will see on this part of the Sinai coast. Some modern restaurants and shopping malls have been added, but essentially this is the old town with small shops on backstreets and an unhurried atmosphere –

A tea shop in Old Sharm

well worth a visit for a couple of hours, especially in the evening.

One of the landmarks of the safe, enclosed bay here is a large tower which gives residents of the Beach Albatros Hotel direct access to the beach. Beyond this is a marvellous clifftop walk with wonderful views along the coast leading out of the bay and around the Ras 'Om Sid headland. The small Sadiki café is popular at sunset, with fine views towards the **Al**

Mustapha Mosque

**Fanar** lighthouse on the headland. Sadly the beach between Sadiki café and the lighthouse is privately owned, so the coastal walk has to be interrupted here. The lighthouse itself gives wonderful views east towards Ras Nasrani and distant Tiran Island, and west to the Ras Muhammad headland. Below the lighthouse is the popular Al Fanar bar and restaurant.

The **Ras 'Om Sid** area, with its many hotels and private beaches, runs from the lighthouse to an isolated rock known as 'The Tower'. The reefs off this coast are popular for diving and snorkelling due to the easy access. Inland is **Hadaba** (meaning 'hill') also with many hotels, resorts and activities centres.

The coastal area between The Tower and Naama Bay is a bit of a scrubby wasteland, but there are large tourist and residential developments along Peace Road, running parallel to the coast about 2km (1¼ miles) inland. The main landmarks here are the twin minarets and dome of the new **Mustapha Mosque** and the twin bell towers and dome of the even newer Coptic Orthodox **Church of St Mary**.

## Naama Bay

This is Sharm's main tourist centre, with crowded shopping malls, tightly packed restaurants and the busiest bars and nightclubs. Since the 2005 bombing, the downtown area of **Naama Bay** has been pedestrianised. This is where most people come to eat outside of their hotel, and many of the surrounding hotels organise free shuttle transfers. From the late afternoon Naama Bay is really buzzing, fuelled by happy-hour offers at many of the bars, some of which have rooftop terraces with great views.

Behind the **Sharm Museum**, which displays glittering replicas of famous Egyptian antiques, is the **Zaza Panorama**, a series of seated terraces cut into the hillside, perfect for that sunset drink. This area is just as lively in the early hours of the morning, as the clubs, casinos and bars are open until 4am or even later – and it's still warm outside.

About 10km (6 miles) further along the coast is **Shark's Bay**, named for the enormous but gentle whale sharks that are frequently seen here. Shark's Bay still retains its local flavour and is a great place for families, with a safe bay for children to play in the water. Between Shark's Bay and the airport is Soho Square (www.soho-sharm.com), a new entertainment complex with ice rink, bowling alley, Culturama historical cinema, nightclubs, international restaurants and bars including the Ice Bar. The 'British House' has a traditional pub named 'The Queen Vic'. Peace Road continues around the airport towards the Nabeq Protectorate.

### Whale sharks

Scuba-divers get very excited about seeing sharks, especially large ones. The largest shark – indeed the largest fish – is a gentle leviathan that can grow to 18m (60ft) in length and only eats plankton. The 2008 summer season was the best ever for sightings, with some divers seeing four whale sharks together.

Sunset in Naama Bay

## Ras Muhammad National Park

At the very southerly tip of Sinai, **Ras Muhammad National Park** (sunrise–sunset; charge) separates the two gulfs and has exceptionally nutrient-rich water flowing in strong currents, attracting fishes of all sizes, especially during the summer months. Great shoals of snapper, jack and tuna can be seen, with large Napoleon wrasse, moray eels and curtains of barracuda. About 15 percent of the fish species seen here are endemic, and the protected underwater coral gardens are truly spectacular in their size, colour and variety.

The turning to the park is 10km (6 miles) west of Sharm El Sheikh on the snaking mountain road, and the entrance gate, made from giant concrete blocks and resembling a collapsed Stonehenge, is a further 10km (6 miles) from here. Entry is strictly controlled to enforce the 'take nothing, leave nothing' ideal. Unless you obtained an Egyptian visa when you arrived at the airport, driving or sailing to Ras

Muhammad takes you out of Sharm El Sheikh territory and into Egypt proper, requiring a visa at US$15. This is not a problem, but it will be added to your bill.

The 480-sq-km (185-sq-mile) national park was formed in 1983, soon after the area was handed back to Egypt by Israel. Since 2003 studies undertaken by the Coral Reef Research Unit and the Egyptian Environmental Affairs Agency (www.eeaa.gov.eg) are examining the effects of tourist damage, fluctuations in sea temperature, coral diseases and pollution on the fragile ecosystems.

Watching the boats arrive at Ras Muhammad between 9am and 10am can be a bit like the D-Day landings, but dives here are memorable. Snorkellers can save a bit of money by travelling by bus or car, but must keep to the marked tracks which provide access to the main sites. Two main headlands reach out to sea with **Hidden Bay** between them. **Quay Beach** and

A tribesman surveys the Mangrove Channel

**Mangrove Channel** are on the western headland, **Yolanda Bay** and **Shark Observatory** are on the eastern headland, and **Yolanda Reef** and **Shark Reef** are just offshore. Yolanda Reef was named after a freighter that sank here in a storm in 1980, discarding hundreds of bathroom sinks and toilets, as well as a BMW. Climb to the top of Shark Observatory to use the free telescope to

Divers at the
Thistlegorm Wreck

search the waters around Shark Reef. This headland is also a favourite spot for migrating birds to linger before continuing their journey.

## Thistlegorm Wreck

The wreck of the English freighter **Thistlegorm** is world-famous within the diving world and can be dived in a long day from Sharm El Sheikh. It lies almost in the middle of the Gulf of Suez, west of Ras Muhammad National Park, and was sunk by German bombers in 1941. The explosion ripped the ship in half, but much of the cargo remains intact, including Norton and BSA motorbikes, tanks, army supplies and even railway engines.

## Tiran Island

**Tiran Island** is situated east of Sharm El Sheikh in the Strait of Tiran. The island belongs to Egypt and controls all access in and out of the Gulf of Aqaba, but is only accessible to the military, because only 12km (7 miles) beyond its easterly towering peak is the mainland of Saudi Arabia.

Wreck of the *Maria Schroeder*

The string of reefs between the island and Ras Nasrani have some remarkable dive sites with an exceptional quality of coral and quantity of large fish. Four main reefs run across the Strait of Tiran – **Gordon, Thomas, Woodhouse** and **Jackson** reefs, all named after British cartographers who first mapped the area 100 years ago.

These protected reefs are some of the most popular diving and snorkelling sites for day boats coming out of Sharm El Sheikh, with as many as 20 boats at each site through the peak season (July–December). To avoid the crowds, try to arrive early (7am–10am) or later in the day. For safety, most dives are on the leeward (southern) sides where there are suitable modern moorings for the boats.

The unusual combination of deep water and narrow passages creates a concentrated, plankton-rich flow of water, which in turn attracts larger fish and their predators – tuna, sailfish and sharks. The best chance of seeing hammerhead sharks between May and August is off the northern end of Jackson Reef. The dangers to shipping are obvious – the *Lara* shipwreck is perched on Jackson Reef and the *Loullia* on Gordon Reef.

## Nabeq Protectorate

Preventing any further development north of Nabeq is the 600-sq-km (230-sq-mile) **Nabeq Protectorate** (Nature Reserve, sunrise–sunset; charge), which stretches along the coastline for over 40km (25 miles). The park's main entry gate is at **Nabeq**, and there are walking trails inside. Several *wadis* drain the mountains, carrying soil and silt to make the area fertile. Roots of dense mangrove trees dig deep into the saltwater marsh flats, providing valuable protection for newly hatched and developing immature fish. Hired taxis can take you inside, but there is a marked landmine area nearby, so they should take care.

Bedouin villages within the protectorate offer traditional handicrafts as souvenirs, and the shallows are fished for clams by local fishermen living in thatched huts. The park's main landmark is the wreck of the **Maria Schroeder**, a ship that grounded itself on the reef in 1956 when sailing from Aqaba to West Germany. The northern half of the protectorate is out of bounds for scientific research and the visitor centre is also closed.

## St Catherine's Monastery

One of the most popular and historically interesting day excursions offered by the tour operators in Sharm El Sheikh is a coach visit to St Catherine's Monastery, tucked below Mount Sinai. The logistics of this day trip are not ideal as the monastery is only open in the mornings, thus requiring a very early start or an overnight stay in the nearby town of St Catherine's. Another option is to visit the monastery on the way down from an over-

St Catherine's Monastery

Part of the ossuary at
St Catherine's Monastery

night climb up Mount Sinai
*(see page 38).*

**St Catherine's Monastery**  **4**

Dayr Sant Katrin (9am–noon, closed Fri, Sun and Greek Orthodox holidays, but sometimes open 11am–noon; free; visitors must dress modestly, with legs and arms covered) is an important biblical site, at the foot of the mountains. Seemingly protected by giant natural walls of rock, it marks the spot where God appeared as a burning bush and spoke to Moses, as described in Chapter 3 of Exodus. The first building on the site was a chapel built around AD330 under the orders of Saint Helena, mother of Constantine, the first Christian Roman emperor, to provide shelter for the hermits who lived in caves close to the Mount Sinai.

The main structures date from the 6th century, when Emperor Justinian paid for an extension (even though he wanted it built on the summit of Mount Sinai), but the rope-and-pulley system once used to haul people over the wall is long gone. The monastery was named after St Catherine, who was born in Alexandria and martyred in the early 4th century, after her body miraculously appeared on a nearby mountain some 300 years after her death.

Despite continual attacks by Bedouins, the sanctuary has survived amazingly well and still functions as a Greek Orthodox monastery with an 11th-century mosque in one of the converted chapels. Some visitors are disappointed to find that large sections of the monastery are closed to the public, but you should always be able to see the **church**, the **Well of Moses** and the still thriving **burning bush**. Great treasures include the church with its 6th-century carved wooden doors, icons and the oldest mosaics of the Eastern Orthodox Church, as well as the illuminated manuscripts in the library. A **visitor centre** (closed Fri; free) further down the valley gives more details about the history of the site.

## Mount Sinai

**Mount Sinai** (known locally as Jabal Musa), where Moses received the Ten Commandments from God, is one of the highest peaks in Egypt at 2,285m (7,497ft). For many Christians, Jews and Muslims this is a very spiritual place. You can gain a greater understanding of the site's significance by reading chapters 19 to 40 of Exodus, which describe Moses' experiences on Mount Sinai.

One of Mount Sinai's rocky paths

In winter it is possible to visit St Catherine's Monastery in the morning and then climb the mountain in the afternoon, witnessing sunset over the mountain peaks, and then descend in the gloom of early evening. This is a long and physically demanding day, but feasible for adults. However, in summer (May to September) the trek to the summit would be too hot in the afternoon, and it is best undertaken as a night climb to witness the spectacular sunrise from the peak. The views from the summit are breathtaking at any time.

From the monastery there are two main routes to climb the 700m (2,300ft) to the summit, both of which children will find difficult. One involves taking a flight of over 3,700 steps called the **Sikkat Saydna Musa** (Path of Moses) that winds its way steeply up a narrow ravine from behind the monastery. It passes through two main gateways: the first is the **Gate of Confession**, built during the reign of Justinian,

Watching the sunrise from Mount Sinai

where a monk would hear pilgrims' confessions so that they arrived at the summit 'with a purified heart'; the second is the **Gate of St Stephen the Anchorite**, who lived as a hermit in a nearby cave. When seen from the monastery in blazing heat, this route is quite daunting.

Church bell on the summit

The other route, which is less steep, continues up the valley past the monastery and winds its way around the side of the mountain. It is called the **Sikkat Al Pasha**, named after Pasha Abbas I, who had the track constructed. It is also known as the camel track, as people can ride almost to the top, dismount and climb just a few hundred steps to the summit. The route has many cafés and rest stops along the way. On special days there might be 1,000 pilgrims making the ascent, but the average is a few hundred.

The most popular combination is to walk up the camel track in about three hours, and then descend by the steps in two hours. In summer this means starting the climb with a guide in the dark at about 2am and arriving back around 9am, with time to visit the monastery after a hugely rewarding breakfast. A night ascent requires a good flashlight, water and a fleece or jacket for the coldness of sunrise at altitude. There can be snow on the mountain in winter.

At the summit is a small **chapel** dedicated to the Holy Trinity, rebuilt in 1934 using stones from earlier destroyed churches, dating back to AD532.

Sunbathing in Dahab

## EASTERN SINAI

The Nabeq Protectorate stops further expansion to the north of Sharm El Sheikh, as does the Ras Abu Ghalum Protectorate further north, but squeezed between them is the pleasant coastal town of Dahab, meaning 'gold'. Further north are some hippie-style beach resorts and the upmarket development of Taba Heights. Inland are remarkable areas of desert and mountain, where you can visit spectacular canyons and traditional Bedouin communities.

### Dahab

**6** Some holidaymakers prefer the casual atmosphere of **Dahab** to the commercialism of Sharm El Sheikh. Many local Bedouin landowners have not sold to large international companies, preferring to invest in their own futures by building smaller family-run hotels that employ local people. Hence

Dahab tends to attract more discerning tourists, with an interest in sustainable tourism, which allows local businesses and shops to thrive.

Dahab's tourist area is known as **Asilah**, which is located about 4km (2½ miles) north of the town's administrative centre. There is public access all of the way along the 3km (1¾ miles) of seafront with its many bars, cafés and restaurants. The excavated ruins at **Al Mashraba Hill**, located at the southern end of Asilah, were uncovered in 1989 and are said to be the remains of a 1st-century-BC Nabataean town, part of a civilisation whose capital was at Petra.

Horses, camels, quad bikes, jeeps and bicycles can all be hired, and a popular excursion is north along the coast into the **Ras Abu Ghalum Protectorate** (sunrise–sunset; free). **⬅7** The protectorate boasts a raised fossilised coral reef and two famous dive sites – the Blue Hole and the Canyon, both of which should be treated with respect. The **Blue Hole** is a remarkable natural circular hole that plunges through the coral reef to a dangerous depth of over 100m (330ft). Attempts to use an 'exit' hole leading out to the reef at 55m (180ft) have caused several diver deaths.

## Nowibe

**Nowibe** (Nuweiba) as one of the early resorts developed during Israeli control due to its proximity to Eilat. Today the hotels are somewhat tired-looking, yet very popular with Eastern Europeans as they offer good value for money. The town is the main administrative centre for the area, but everything here seems to revolve around the little port and its ferries to and from Aqaba. There are two ferries (fast and slow) in each direction daily, both leaving in the mid-afternoon. Nowibe is losing out to other resorts as the reefs are not as good this far north. The best parts of town are north of the centre in the **Tarabin** suburb, where there is an Ottoman fort.

North of Nowibe are several laid-back resorts in stunning locations, most consisting of a few thatched beach huts with few other facilities. Visitors tend to spend months here rather than days, chilling out and relaxing at the local pace of life, where the biggest hassle is ordering another beer or smoke. If you want to drop out, if only for a few days, try **Maagana Beach**, **Castle Beach** at Ras Al Shaytan, the eco-resort **Basata** or **Bir Swair**.

## Coloured Canyon

Between Dahab and Taba, one of the easiest and most popular excursions is to Coloured Canyon, a wonderfully eroded small gorge. You will need the assistance of a local guide, and permission is required to pass through the checkpoint on the road up **Wadi Watir** that runs directly inland from Nowibe and eventually leads to Suez and Cairo. Geological upheavals

Climbing through the Coloured Canyon

can be seen all around, with some of the rock strata now almost vertical. **Ain Al Fortagah** is a natural spring by the roadside in the steep-sided gorge, around which a few palm trees grow. From here a track leads north around some farms to reach an escarpment after 40 minutes' rough 4x4 driving.

From a local Bedouin café a steep footpath drops for 15 minutes down through brilliant white rocks to the foot of Jabal Arada and into the **Coloured Canyon**. The canyon slowly narrows and snakes left and right, and the sandy *wadi* floor is sometimes only wide enough to fit one shoe in front of the other. The rock faces on either side are naturally carved into weird and wonderful shapes, coloured red, cream and ochre. Some boulders have crashed down from above, obstructing the way, and need to be squeezed under, and there are a couple of drops of a metre or so that you must scramble down. You need good footwear and to be fairly agile, but some tourists have turned back having found a boulder too large to fit underneath. The canyon hike takes about 30 minutes and the whole trek about an hour, so there is plenty of time to go further with your 4x4.

About 30 minutes west is **Wadi Huweiyit**, a large valley full of towering sand dunes and easy to climb rock faces. Traces of ancient habitation and early trade can be seen at old wells such as **Bir Al Biyariya**.

## Ain Khodrah

Returning to Ain Al Fortagah, another track goes due south along Wadi Ghazala. After 30km (18 miles) of tough 4x4 driving you arrive at **Ain Khodrah**, generally accepted as the place mentioned in both the Bible and Torah as part of the route Moses and his followers took after they left Mount Sinai. The fact that anything grows here seems a miracle, but thanks to a small spring there are extensive palm, olive, lemon and fig trees supporting three Bedouin families. This small

Camel at Ain Khodrah

tribal community is helped by a few eco-friendly adventure companies which bring tourists here for lunch or an overnight stay, whilst respecting their lifestyle *(see page 89)*. The tribespeople supply visitors with tea and food, and sell locally made handicrafts. The extra income that this provides is very important and allows them to remain here rather than move to the coast as many others have done. Thursday night is the main Bedouin wedding night, and visitors are welcomed if they happen upon one of these traditional tribal celebrations.

There are also two trekking routes from Ain Khodrah – the ancient Moses trail and an interesting walk through the **White Canyon** that leads back to Wadi Ghazala. It is possible to see desert foxes, wild goats and gazelles (after which the valley is named), but a local guide must always be taken as it is easy to get hopelessly lost in this area.

Wadi Ghazala eventually reaches the road to St Catherine's from the coast. Beyond a small UN camp off the road to St Catherine's are some remarkable Bronze Age ruins, called the **Nawamis Tombs**. Built on a small ridge below **Jabal Matamir** are over 20 ancient burial tombs, constructed from rough stones, dating to around 3500BC. Nearby are smooth exposed rocks covered with carvings and inscriptions showing that this has long been a trading and pilgrimage route between Mount Sinai and the head of the Gulf of Aqaba – and therefore between Jerusalem and St Catherine's Monastery.

## Taba Heights and Jazurat Fer'un

**Taba Heights** is the Eastern Sinai's answer to Al Gunah resort near Hughadah – a purpose-built tourist complex of a few upmarket resorts sharing a coastline, marina, golf course and other facilities. The setting, between the tranquil turquoise waters of the Gulf of Aqaba and the towering red mountains nearby, is certainly spectacular. Several airlines now fly direct to Taba airport, allowing tourists to avoid a long transfer from Sharm El Sheikh. To the north of Taba Heights the road swings inland, obscuring the view of the **Sun Pool**, an unusual natural lake isolated from the sea. The road then rejoins the coast at the beautiful inlet known as the **Fjord**, one of the best natural harbours in the Gulf of Aqaba for small boats.

**11** ▶

**12** ▶    **Jazurat Fer'un** (Pharaoh's Island, also known as Saladin's Island and Coral Island; sunrise–sunset; boat and admission charge) is the furthest south that T.E. Lawrence and Sir Leonard Wooley explored during their archaeological survey covering the 'Wilderness of Zin' (Sinai) in 1913 *(see box below)*. They noted that Jazurat Fer'un is known by several names, but that the Crusaders always referred to it as Graye. Despite the notices today saying that everything dates from Saladin's Ayyubid pe-

Bedouin woman making bread

## Lawrence of Arabia

T.E. Lawrence gained much expert local knowledge through his travels in the 'Wilderness of Zin' in 1913, during which he visited Jazurat Fer'un *(pictured above)*. His knowledge proved valuable in World War I, when he led the Arab Revolt against the Turks, taking Aqaba Fort. Through his heroic exploits he became known as 'Lawrence of Arabia'.

riod (late 12th century), Lawrence noted that 'the whole of the north half of the fort is more like 15th- or 16th-century work, repaired in the 18th century'. They also describe the small mosque (the door of which is closed at present) and how the plain plastered *mihrab* had been covered in graffiti by visiting sailors of HMS *Diana* in 1896.

Today there is more to be seen than at their visit, due to the ongoing modern repairs to the bathhouse, granary, kitchen, cisterns and walls. The island's small inlet may have been King Solomon's harbour for Hiram's Phoenician ships, as mentioned in the Bible. Access is by boat across the incredibly clear waters.

The small village of **Taba**  is an enclave of a few shops and administrative buildings right on the border with Israel. They service the border crossing and the Hilton Hotel, which is still popular with Israeli tourists.

# WESTERN SINAI

The present Sharm El Sheikh conurbation is referred to as Sharm I, but northwest of Ras Muhammad National Park is a large empty coastline identified as Sharm II – the next huge area earmarked for future development. Western Sinai's coastline is connected with the oil industry, but the area also has an ancient history dating right back to pharaonic times.

## At Tur

The capital of South Sinai is the modern town of **At Tur**, which  initially looks to be of little interest. It originally developed as the port closest to St Catherine's monastery, which is less than 50km (30 miles) away. Excavations are continuing at the site of the old **Raithou Monastery**, where food and supplies were stored before being carried up to St Catherine's. At Tur must also have been an important port in later years, as the oldest known reference to the coffee trade was found in a letter here, written in 1497. Some of the town's Ottoman-period houses are in a very poor state, but there is an interesting area of traditional boat-building and repair, as well as a modern industry fitting out dive boats for the main resorts.

Traditional boat-building, At Tur

A small road runs north along the coast for 3km (1¾ miles) to a natural spring known as the **Bath of Moses** (8am–sunset; charge). There are indoor and outdoor pools for taking the sulphurous waters, said to be good for rheumatic treatment and curing skin diseases. A terrace restaurant and café are locat-

The Bath of Moses

ed up the hillside and are popular with locals, offering wonderful views across the Gulf at sunset.

## Wadi Firan and Wadi Al Mokattab

Around 66km (41 miles) further along this road, a right turn leads up **Wadi Firan**, the main modern road from the west coast to St Catherine's. About 22km (13 miles) along this road, a wide valley enters from the north, which has been a major thoroughfare for thousands of years. Known as **Wadi Al Mokattab** (meaning 'Valley of Writing'), it has many inscriptions made by Bedouin traders and religious pilgrims, and was probably part of the route taken by Moses and his followers. This is the shortest route to St Catherine's and Mount Sinai if travelling from Suez. All the neighbouring *wadis* have similar inscriptions, even as far north as the turquoise mines around Sarabet Al Khadem *(see page 50)*. As well as the many inscriptions, the entire area is a geologist's dream, with exposed seabeds still showing ripples of coastal sand, frozen in time since the final tide went out. The *wadi* is extremely difficult to find, being something of a 'hidden valley', and requires a 4x4 and local guide. Sadly, some modern visitors have scratched their own names onto the rocks.

Further east, Wadi Firan opens up into a fine palmery known as the **Oasis of Firan** with many date palms along the roadside, shading the local houses. The village of **Tarfah** is said to be the location of the 'manna from heaven' as described in Exodus chapter 16, *manna* being a tiny white nourishing deposit produced on tamarisk bushes. For the truly adventurous, the hills and mountains here provide excellent trekking through Mazeena tribal land all the way to Nowibe, but again, only with fully equipped local guides.

## Sarabet Al Khadem Temple

Back on the coastal road is the prosperous modern oil town of **Abu Radis**, the centre of Western Sinai's oil industry, with many offshore rigs. Just before the port of **Abu Znimah** is an inland road that accesses new ore mines, but this area also has some of the oldest mines in Egypt. It was exploited by the early pharaohs for its useful copper and attractive turquoise – extremely popular as jewellery in ancient times. The presence of cop-

### Wadi Al Mokattab

Analysis of the various scripts has suggested a link between ancient Egyptian hieroglyphics and the Ugaritic alphabet used in the 14th century BC in nearby Syria, from which our own alphabet developed.

Ancient carvings at Sarabet Al Khadem Temple

per gives turquoise its distinctive greenish-blue colour and also produces a mineral called malachite, which has a rich green colour used as a cosmetic. The landscape is a strange mixture of surreal white weathered mountains and sweeping brown desert plateaux.

 One of the most remarkable buildings in Sinai is **Sarabet Al Khadem Temple** (sunrise–sunset; free). This ancient Egyptian temple, complete with ceremonial entranceway, pylon, courtyard and inner sanctuary, dates from around 2700BC to 1100BC. It seems to have had a double function – it is dedicated to the goddess Hathor, who is referred to here as 'the lady of the turquoise', but also glorifies the power of the pharaohs who commanded the mining expeditions into such remote and inhospitable locations. Excavations have unearthed a relief of King Snefru (now in the Egyptian Museum in Cairo) indicating ancient activity here at least as far back as the building of the Giza pyramids

4,500 years ago. Later pharaohs also wanted to keep the precious ores flowing and dedicated other chapels, statues and inscribed steles. The site, which bends around its axis to fit onto the hillside, is quite small and in a ruined condition, but it is a remarkable find in such a remote location. Dug into the hillside on which the temple stands are the remains of the old quarries and mines that once provided the turquoise.

The excursion from Abu Znimah takes at least six hours, and the temple can only be found with a local guide and 4x4. The temple is finally reached after an hour's walk up a small pass called **Rod Al Air** (meaning 'track of the little donkey') that has been used for thousands of years, as witnessed by the wonderful Middle and New Kingdom-period carvings on its exposed rocks. Ancient artists depicted wild animals such as giraffes and a whole fleet of sailing craft with oars that carried the minerals. Their harbour was at **Markhah** (7km/4 miles south of modern Abu Znimah), where the turquoise was loaded and shipped across the Gulf of Suez.

Another three hours of 4x4 driving further east of the temple, in a location about as remote as you can get in the central Sinai, are a strange set of weathered rocks known as the **Jabal Fugah** rock pillars. A desert safari of several days could  link all of these unusual sites, together with Wadi Mokattab and St Catherine's *(see page 89).*

## Northern Gulf of Suez

North of Abu Znimah the coastal road swings inland around Jabal Hammam Fer'un, which rises to almost 500m (1,640ft). At the foot of this mountain, where it drops into the sea, is an outpouring of hot sulphurous water from a natural hot water spring known as **Hammam Fer'un** (Pharaoh's Bath).

A small cave overlooking the sea gives access inside the

## Hammam Fer'un

Local Bedouins say that the hot springs are named in memory of the cursed Pharaoh whose army was drowned crossing the Red Sea whilst chasing Moses. Being very superstitious, they also say that his worried soul still haunts the cave and mountain.

mountain, which soon becomes a natural sauna surrounded by the hot rocks. The humidity increases further inside the final tunnel, which can only be reached on hands and knees and is a truly sweating experience. Many locals come here for the treatment of skin and eye diseases. Those not wanting to go caving simply relax and float in the warm, shallow sea waters, as the hot springs also seep up through the seabed. It is a popular site for weekend outings from Cairo and picnics for many local families, often with a party atmosphere.

Between here and Suez oil production is inland rather than offshore, allowing the coast around **Ras Sedr** to once again become an adventure-sports paradise. The coral growth is not as good this far north, but the reef is close to shore, giving easy access. The main natural attraction here is the strong coastal winds, which are harnessed for wind- and kitesurfing. Resorts such as **Moon Beach** are dedicated to these sports, with near-perfect conditions every day. This 40km (25-mile) stretch of coastline is home to some of the largest building projects, but it all seems eerily empty. The closeness to Cairo and the other Delta cities is the main attraction for the many Egyptian second-home properties.

Many ships wait in this part of the Gulf of Suez to enter the Suez Canal. Within sight of the large tower at the canal's entrance is another location with biblical connections. **Ain Musa** (the Spring of Moses) is set behind a local roadside café in a somewhat unkempt oasis of palms. After crossing the Red Sea the Israelites are said to have drunk here from

12 springs among 70 palm trees before entering the Wilderness of Zin and reaching Mount Sinai.

Today the site is somewhat disappointing, with two wells (one of which is usually dry and full of rubbish) and heavy trucks roaring past. The local tourist police can take you to another five wells situated just further north, but the first two seem more than enough. Also just to the north of here beside the main road is the **Musa Fortified Firing Position** – a memorial to the place from where the Israelis shelled Suez prior to 1973.

Several roads run eastwards from the top of the Gulf of Suez, crossing Central and Northern Sinai. The main road, which carries a regular bus service linking Suez with Taba, passes through **Nakhl** and **Ath Thammad**, and has always been an important route between the heads of both gulfs. This is the main overland road from Cairo to Mecca, and has been used by millions of pilgrims over the years. It was also the route by which the exhausted Lawrence of Arabia travelled by camel in the opposite direction between Aqaba and Cairo, to let his army superiors know that his Arab Revolt had taken Aqaba Fort from the Turks in July 1917.

Access from Sinai to the city of Suez and the rest of

One of the wells at Ain Musa

Egypt is through the **Ahmad Hamdi Tunnel**, named after an Egyptian engineer killed in the 1973 war. It was originally built by the British in 1983, but within the first decade of use serious repairs had to be carried out by a Japanese company. The tunnel is still not without its leakage problems, despite being 37m (121ft) below the canal.

# GULF OF SUEZ

The western branch of the northern Red Sea is named after the area's main port, Suez, the southern terminus of the Suez Canal. It is very much a working port city, however, and there

## The Parting of the Red Sea

The image of Moses raising his arms to part the Red Sea is one of the most famous of biblical stories. The account relates how Moses led the Jewish slaves out of Egypt pursued by Pharaoh's army (Exodus 13–15). Having arrived at the Red Sea, they were trapped until Moses parted the waves to allow the Israelites to walk along the seabed between walls of water. Reaching the other side Moses closed the sea again, trapping the pursuing Egyptians and drowning their entire army.

This miracle, like many biblical stories – such as the 10 plagues of Egypt – might now be possible to explain with our modern understanding of natural phenomena. Three major events could potentially have caused the Red Sea to part – a tsunami, an earthquake (or volcanic eruption) and wind setdown. The first two are usually dismissed due to the short amount of time that the seabed is exposed, but a strong enough wind (as also described in Exodus) might force back the sea as a wall of water.

However, experts cannot even agree about the location of the crossing, whether it is the Gulf of Aqaba or the Gulf of Suez, which also places in doubt the exact location of Mount Sinai.

is little here to detain tourists for long. Even so, the area's history is fascinating – it has been an important destination for mariners, merchants, pilgrims and other travellers for thousands of years.

## Suez (Asswayss)

It was the Egyptian pharaohs who first recognised the strategic importance of the **Suez** area, at the head of the Gulf of Suez and close to Egypt's most populous regions. Around 1850BC they are said to have built an east–west canal linking the Gulf to the Nile here. Two ports grew up, Clysma (on the site of modern Suez city) and, a few kilometres away,

A large ship passes Badr Mosque in Suez

Arsinoe, named after the wife of Ptolemy II, ruler of Egypt in the 3rd century BC. Clysma prospered towards the end of the Roman period when ports further south in the Red Sea, once favoured by traders over northern ports because of the prevailing winds, came under constant attack by Bedouin tribes. Even though Clysma was difficult to reach by sail from the south, it remained an important port into the Islamic period (from the 7th century AD), when it was known as Qulzum. The area continued to be a crossroads for pilgrims and traders between Alexandria and India, Cairo and Jerusalem, Constantinople and Yemen. Spices and coffee were shipped northwards, and Muslim pilgrims regularly travelled

Ship sailing through the desert on the Suez Canal

to and from Mecca, via the Arabian port of Jeddah.

Suez was the base of the Ottoman sailor and cartographer Piri Reis, who secured the whole of the Red Sea for the Ottomans when he sailed south and recaptured Aden in Yemen from the Portuguese in 1549. His 'world map', dating from 1513, is now preserved in the Topkapı Library in İstanbul. At about this time, the Red Sea and Gulf of Suez became marginalised as European navigators found a direct route to the Indies around Africa. Apart from local Ottoman trade, all exotic eastern goods bypassed the Red Sea after the 16th century.

Today it is difficult to make a case for Suez being anything other than a transit stop. It is a place in which everyone seems to be going somewhere else – soldiers on the move from Sinai, tourists visiting Cairo and the Nile, and pilgrims going to and from Mecca, Jerusalem, St Catherine's or the desert monasteries. And there is not much of antiquity to be seen – Israeli bombardments flattened the city following the 1967 war, and the old buildings were replaced by blocks of tenements.

## Suez Canal

The Red Sea once again became an important maritime trading route with the building of the **Suez Canal** by the Belgian engineer Ferdinand de Lesseps. A great 19th-century techno-logical achievement, the canal took 10 years to build, opening in 1869. It linked the Red Sea with the Mediterranean via Ismailia and Port Said, assuring Suez's future and dramatically cutting the shipping route between East and West – halving the distance between Bombay and London, for example.

Suez city is the canal's southern terminus, and its harbour is at **Port Tewfik** (Boar Tewfik), an artificial peninsula where the canal meets the Gulf of Suez. This pleasant garden suburb is the best place to view the canal. A wonderful esplanade runs along the side of the canal, with **Badr Mosque** at one end. Elsewhere around Suez it is not possible to reach the coast or canal due to oil refineries, as well as the high level of military security presence.

Each day, scores of ships line up in the gulf ready to make the northward passage, starting at 7am. The modern canal is 192km (119 miles) long with no locks, and about 10 percent of the world's shipping uses it, taking about 16 hours to pass through. The southbound convoy usually arrives in Suez about 3pm, and for a couple of hours the giant container ships and empty oil tankers silently slip into the warm waters of the Red Sea. Despite recent improvements to the canal, some of the very largest ships are excluded, due to the 70m (230ft) clearance below the road bridge at Al Qantarah and the 16m (52ft) draught limit. The authorities are sensitive about visitors taking photographs of the canal and ships.

South from Suez along the western coast of the gulf are seemingly endless industrial zones, smelly petrochemical plants and dusty quarries. About 55km (34 miles) south of Suez is **Al' in As Sokhnah**

## Coffee ships

During the Ottoman coffee boom in the late 18th century it is said that the cost of building a coffee-trading ship could be recovered with just three journeys between Suez and Jeddah.

Church towers at the
Monastery of St Anthony

('hot spring'), a modern port terminal at the end of the shortest road between Cairo and the Red Sea. One of the largest hotel projects in Egypt is **Porto Sokhnah** – a series of high-rise buildings set back from pleasant beaches – aimed at the Egyptian second-home market. The area has seen significant changes in recent years, and there are now hundreds of wind turbines harnessing the wind to power the new resorts. Despite these developments, the old way of life has not entirely disappeared, and you can sometimes see the curving lines of traditional fish traps laid out in the clear shallow waters.

## Monastery of St Anthony

A main road at **Az Za'faranah** runs from the coast to Bani Swaif on the Nile, along which tourist vehicles are allowed to travel between 6am and 6pm. It is also the road used to access the **Monastery of St Anthony** (9am–5pm, closed during Lent and Christmas; entry and guides free but donations welcome), known locally as Dayr Al Qeddis Antun, about 50km (31 miles) from Az Za'faranah.

The approach to the monastery is through a wilderness of sun-bleached rocks and rugged folded mountains. This is exactly what 'the father of monasticism' St Anthony was looking for when he retreated here for complete solitude. He was born in Upper Egypt in the middle of the 3rd century AD and lived for over 100 years. A great miracle-worker and protective saint, his life was recorded by Athanasius and his temptations became the subject of many works of religious art over the centuries. Halfway through his life he became a hermit, living in a cave high up the cliff face. Early Christian followers escaping persecution settled at the foot of the mountain, forming the first hermitage in Egypt, and the country's largest monastery subsequently developed. Thanks to its remoteness, the community was spared during the arrival of Islam, but it has always suffered from Bedouin raids.

The oldest part of the complex is the **church** built over St Anthony's tomb, which dates from the 6th century and is full of impressive frescoes. There are other small church-

## Visiting the Monasteries

Remember to bring your passport, as there is a check at the main gateway to each monastery. When arriving at St Anthony's or St Paul's monastery, go straight to the information office, where it is possible to get a guided tour by one of the fathers who speak English. Otherwise wander around, but some of the doors and churches are locked at various times. Both monasteries can be crowded with Coptic pilgrims, but if you tell the guardians that you have travelled from overseas, they will sometimes let you into 'closed' areas. At St Paul's it is even possible to briefly meet Abuna Fanous, said to have remarkable healing powers and hands which illuminate when he is reading the liturgy.

Technically it is possible to spend the night at the monasteries, but permission must be obtained in advance from the Church headquarters in Cairo (tel: 02-2590 0218).

es here looked after by the 70 monks, one of whom used to be chosen as a representative to the Ethiopian Coptic Church until 1951. A natural water spring supplies the monastery allowing the monks to grow palm and olive trees.

It is possible to go around the back of the monastery and climb the steps up to the original **cave** where St Anthony lived. Take plenty of water as this 45-minute climb up 300m (1,000ft) of rock-cut and metal steps is tough in the heat of the day, especially for the very young and old. The views from the cave terrace are magnificent, but it is a very narrow squeeze into the cave itself. At the back, just where the sunlight disappears are a few steps down to the memorial where St Anthony resided. You will need to take a flashlight with you otherwise you will end up groping around in the darkness. You should also take extra care

The New Church at the Monastery of St Paul

descending the mountain, as the steps are irregular and uneven.

The Monastery of St Paul is only about 20km (12 miles) away across the mountains as the crow flies, but the road journey to get there is almost 100km (62 miles) back through Az Za'faranah.

A Coptic monk

## Monastery of St Paul

**23** The **Monastery of St Paul** (9am–5pm except Lent and Christmas; entry and guides free but donations welcome), known locally as Dayr Al Qeddis Bulos, is reached along a road that turns off the coastal road 25km (15 miles) south of Za Farana. This St Paul (not the Apostle) was born in Thebes in the 2nd century AD and so slightly predates St Anthony. St Paul also lived in a cave, becoming the first known Christian hermit, but according to their histories, St Paul is said to have acknowledged that his neighbour – the younger St Anthony – was his spiritual superior. The original church dates from the 5th century, inside which is a white marble sarcophagus said to contain St Paul's body on the site of his cave. The monastery now has four churches, a canteen, a central tower and the monks' private quarters, but is altogether smaller than St Anthony's.

South of Az Za'faranah is **Ras Gharib**. This was originally a small port at the end of an access route through the mountains to the Nile, but it is now concerned with oil extraction and production.

Al Gunah's marina is lined with luxury yachts

## HURGHADAH AND AL GUNAH

The largest tourist centre on Egypt's Red Sea coast is Hurghadah (Al Ghardaqah). Being just outside the Gulf of Suez, the corals grow well, attracting marvellous marine life. This is the fun centre of Egypt, where you sometimes have to remind yourself that you are in a Muslim country.

There is little history to the coast here, but it is possible to make excursions to some of ancient Egypt's greatest sites in the Nile Valley – Luxor (Al Uqsur) is only four hours' drive from Hurghadah. A single long day allows just enough time to see Luxor's main highlights – the Valley of the Kings, Queen Hatshepsut's Temple and Karnak Temple. By staying overnight you can also add Luxor Temple, the sound-and-light show at Karnak and even an early-morning balloon flight over the Nile.

A trip to Cairo to see the Giza pyramids, Sphinx and Egyptian Museum takes about six hours each way. An overnight stay allows time for visits to the Citadel and mosques of Old Cairo. Internal flights are sometimes possible, but most people opt to travel by luxury coach, although these can be very long days, leaving early in the morning and arriving back late at night. The road is now open 24 hours for tourist vehicles.

## Al Gunah

One of the most dramatic and pleasant tourist developments in the area is the huge **Al Gunah** project about  20km (12 miles) north of Hurghadah, now one of the Red Sea's premier destinations. The vision of an Egyptian entrepreneur, it was planned as a self-contained community served by its own little airstrip, where everything would be done at an easy pace, to a high standard. A series of natural and man-made lagoons break up the coastline into small islands and peninsulas, whilst lush gardens and an 18-hole golf course designed to USPGA standards by Fred Couples and Gene Bates have been skilfully landscaped out of the barren desert sands. Wealthy Egyptians, Gulf Arabs and Europeans have bought the expensive beachfront villas, whilst visitors can stay in one of the many attractive hotels ranging from three to five stars.

The centre of town, known as **Kafr Al Gunah**, is packed with shopping arcades, restaurants and bars. The resort's infrastructure also includes horse-riding stables, a go-kart track, cycle routes, a casino and all the usual water-sports facilities. If you want everything on tap and have little

### Roman games

Al Gunah now covers the ancient harbour of Abu Sha'r, which at one point was protected by a Roman fort. Excavations have uncovered board games and even a gaming room, where no doubt the bored soldiers whiled away their time.

Visiting the mosque in Ad Dahar

interest in what lies outside, Al Gunah is perfect, otherwise, Hurghadah offers more in the way of activities and nightlife.

## Hurghadah

The development of this town in the last two decades has been incredible, and there seems to be no end to the amount of expansion both north and south. **Hurghadah** (Al Ghardaqah) ◄ **25** can now be regarded as three separate suburbs – the old downtown (known as Ad Dahar), the new downtown (now called Sakala) and the developed strip running south along the coast for over 20km (12 miles), known as New Hurghadah.

To the north, **Ad Dahar** has some of the earliest hotels and resorts that sprung up between the Jabal Al Afish hill **A** ► and the sea. The **Red Sea Aquarium** (6 Corniche Street; daily 9am–10pm, closed Fri for prayers; charge) on the coast gives non-divers a great opportunity to observe the Red Sea's rich marine life close-up, including sharks, turtles and stonefish. Between Ad Dahar and Sakala are the remnants of what Hurghadah used to be – a public beach, naval dockyards, fishing harbour and port from where the ferry to Sharm El Sheikh departs.

**B** ► Continuing south, **Sakala** suddenly bursts into view with resorts, shops and restaurants running along its main street, off which are roads to the beaches. Here are the Western fast food and retail outlets favoured by many of the tourists who come here, and the usual souvenir shops filled with leather items, brasswork, papyrus and furry camels. In the daytime the modern centre of Hurghadah is not a particularly pretty sight, and the small public beaches are sometimes littered with rubbish. The ambitious **Hurghada Marina Boulevard** (www.hurghadamarinaredsea.com) project, opened in 2008, is designed to regenerate the central beach area with shops, restaurants and a marina. At night the whole area comes alive with pubs, restaurants, beach bars and nightclubs such as Ministry of Sound, Hedkandi and Papas, and the calls of the muezzin have to battle it out with Madonna and Moby.

The main **Sheraton Road** rejoins the coast and climbs 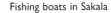 past the Felfela restaurant to reach the abandoned circular Sheraton Hotel, beyond which are endless upmarket resorts catering for the modern beach-loving tourist. The

Fishing boats in Sakala

long paved **promenade** running from the Sindbad Club area southwards is a wonderful safe area, bordered by shops and restaurants.

Protected by offshore islands, the water around Hurghadah is warm all the year round except for a few weeks in December and January. Even in the hottest summer months there is a good breeze, which can sometimes turn into a strong wind, affecting dive-boat destinations and ferry timetables. Every water sport is available – scuba-diving, snorkelling, sailing, kite- and windsurfing.

The best daily dive sites are beyond the islands protecting Hurghadah's coast. Off the eastern coast of **Little Giftun Island** is Erg Somaya, which has beautiful coral gardens and many small fish, as well as Gorgonia Reef, with some large fan corals. To the south of Little Giftun Island is Halg, with many shoals of larger fish. Further

## The Sadana Wreck

One protected dive site that it is not possible to visit is the wreck of a huge 18th-century trading vessel that sank off the Sadana Islands, just to the southeast of Hurghadah. It was carrying an exotic mixture of goods and must have been sailing north towards Suez, as its main cargo consisted of unroasted coffee beans from the Yemeni port of Mocha. Other items on board were Indian pepper, spices, coconuts and oyster shells.

Interestingly, there were no cannons found on the 900-ton vessel, probably because the ship only sailed in the northern Red Sea under the complete protection of the Ottoman Empire, with no threat from European ships or pirates. The ship's design remains a mystery, but possibly originates from an Indian ship-building yard.

The wrecks of three other massive cargo ships from roughly the same period exist in the northern Red Sea, but looting and disturbance by earlier divers have made them virtually useless for underwater archaeology.

There are some spectacular dive sites around Hurghadah

south in an area known as the **Aquarium** is Gota Abu Ramada, which is a beautiful shallow dive of around 12m
(40ft), with many jacks and barracudas. To the north is
**Carless Reef**, which was one of the top dive sites, famous
for sharks and large moray eels, until about 15 years ago
when it succumbed to over-diving. It has only recently
begun to recover. Beyond the range of the daily dive boats
are some of the best dive sites in the world, reached by
'liveaboards' or by travelling along the coast and taking a
boat from another harbour.

Those who want to explore the waters without getting
wet can try the Seascope Semi-Submarine and Sindbad Submarine *(see page 88)*, which make several trips daily to view
the underwater world. For sport fisherman, all-day or
overnight fishing trips to the offshore islands can be arranged
either through the hotels, or privately with individual boat
owners at the harbour.

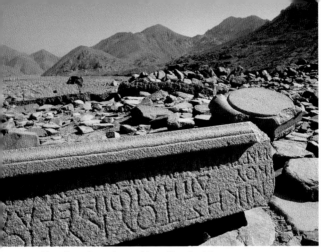

Abandoned carving at Mons Porphyritis

## Mons Porphyritis

In pharaonic times the mountainous Eastern Desert was exploited for gold and other precious materials and ornamental stone. Thousands of prisoners were forced to extract these riches, and many died in the mines and quarries. Gold was dug out and smelted, and both granite and limestone were quarried and transported to Thebes for the construction of temples and other monuments. These resources contributed greatly to the wealth and prestige of the pharaohs and were later coveted by Assyrians, Persians, Greeks and Romans.

The Romans established permanent quarrying camps in the mountains and particularly valued the purplish-red stone called porphyry found at **Mons Porphyritis** (Mountain of Porphyry) below Jabal Abu Dokh Khan (meaning 'Father of Smoke'). According to Pliny the Elder this 'imperial porphyry' stone was discovered at this single location in AD18, and great blocks were quarried then dragged along the Via Porphyritis to Qena, from where they were transported down the Nile and on to Rome. The largest columns were used to build the great temple at Heliopolis (now Baalbek in modern Lebanon), but eight of these were later moved to Constantinople to support the roof of the great Hagia Sophia church. Emperor Hadrian built a small **temple** here, but the whole quarry was abandoned by the 5th century. All that remains are roughly hewn columns, half-inscribed blocks and a ruined fort.

It is sometimes a decade between rainfalls here, and water supply has always been a problem, as witnessed by the many cisterns and channels dug into the bed of **Wadi 'Om Sidri**, named after the Sidri trees which somehow manage to grow here. The route along the *wadi* to Mons Porphyritis is a fascinating, if slow and bumpy journey, through major land upheavals where geology is laid bare, and takes at least two hours each way from Hurghadah. Access is only by 4x4, and an expert driver and guide are needed to find the correct route of the countless desert tracks now only used by the Ma'aza tribe (*see page 89*).

## Coastal Resorts between Hurghadah and Safajah

The development at **Sahl Hashish** has many large resort hotels, each with their own expansive beaches. **Makadi Bay**  is a well-protected natural arc of coastline further south and location of the new dolphin show (www.dolphinworld-egypt.com). Diving here is in its infancy, with many pristine reefs just off the shore, and some dive boats come here from Hurghadah for the deep drop-offs. These new resorts provide an almost continuous string of developments towards **Sharm Al Nagah**, a protected inlet that is also a popular destination for visiting divers and snorkellers.

Further south, near Safajah, is **Soma Bay** (www.soma bay.com) with three top-class resorts and the Gary Player-designed Cascades championship golf course. Deep-sea fishing is good from here, and several new dive centres have opened, offering trips to the Panorama and Abu Kafan sites, which both have impressive reef walls.

# PORT SAFAJAH AND AL QASIR

South of Hurghadah is 700km (435 miles) of coastline to explore before the border with Sudan. This is still an area of unspoilt coastal villages and harsh mountain landscapes. There is some development around Safajah, but for the most part there are endless sandy beaches and gorgeous turquoise seas, where adventurous divers are always searching for new sites.

## Port Safajah

This port developed at the end of the shortest route through the mountains to the River Nile at Qena, and as such could be one of the oldest on the Red Sea. The port is protected by

## The Salem Express Tragedy

On the night of 15 December 1991 in the midst of a severe storm the *Salem Express* ferry was returning from Jeddah to Safajah heavily loaded with cargo and hundreds of pilgrims from Mecca. Less than an hour from safety she hit the Hyndman reef and sank almost immediately just after midnight. No lifeboats were launched, and the continuing storm meant that rescuing survivors was extremely difficult. Several hundred people lost their lives, and even though all bodies were subsequently removed by the Egyptian navy, there are many personal possessions still on board.

The ship now lies on its side with the upper part only 12m (40ft) from the surface, so it is an easy dive. At present there is no ban on diving this wreck, and it is up to each diver to decide if it feels appropriate to dive on such a modern wreck with its associated great loss of life.

Friendly faces in Port Safajah

Safajah Island, and in Islamic times it became the main transit point for pilgrimage crossings to Mecca and Medina.

Modern **Safajah** has only recently encouraged tourism, and its main sources of income have included phosphate extraction and a large naval base. In the almost permanent windy conditions windsurfing is very popular, and the town hosted the world championships in 1993. Just 15km (9 miles) south of Safajah is the wreck of the *Salem Express* ferry *(see page 70)*.

Around 22km (13 miles) south of the modern town is the ancient harbour of **Marsa Gawasis**, from where the Middle and New Kingdom Egyptians sailed to the Land of Punt. During the reign of Ptolemy II this port was called Philoteras and was one of the most important on the entire coast. Recent excavations have uncovered a series of five parallel rock-cut rooms in the fossilised coral terrace, originally sited along the seashore but now some distance inland. Finds inside the caves include large planks of cedar for shipbuilding and coils of

Mons Claudianus

ship's rope, just as they were left thousands of years ago. A carved stele dates from the reign of Amenhotep I around 1900BC, as do hand-painted wooden boxes mentioning 'the wonderful things of Punt'. Oak from Southwest Asia indicates trade links at least 4,000 years ago.

## Mons Claudianus

The quarries at **Mons Claudianus** (Mountain of Emperor Claudius) were used to obtain a high-quality quartzy diorite granite, which found its way all over the Roman Empire. Many structures in Rome built under the emperors Nero, Trajan and Hadrian, including the Pantheon, Temple of Venus and Hadrian's Villa, as well as the later public baths of Caracalla, have architectural elements made from this stone. Today the quarry is reached via the main road between Safajah and Qena, but only attempt this with a 4x4 and a local guide.

At the checkpoint just outside Safajah on the road towards Qena, the police might inspect your passport, so make sure to carry it with you. After 41km (25 miles) a new road has been constructed northwards to Suhag on the Nile and gives easy 4x4 access to Mons Claudianus after 20km (12 miles). Sections of broken tarmac road alongside are remains of the old British-built road linking Qena with Hurghadah, but access is not currently allowed from Hurghadah.

Ruins of the Roman town for the workers and guards lie in the bed of a small *wadi*, around which are scattered columns and blocks, extracted from the quarries but never removed. Defensive towers indicate that the site must have come under attack from local Bedouin tribesmen at times. Eroded tracks all over the hillsides connect open quarries, each with their telltale oblong niches where huge blocks of stone were prized from the mountainside. This is much more extensive, interesting and easier to get to than Mons Porphyritis, which is not much further north, but accessible only from Hurghadah.

## Al Qasir

**Al Qasir** is a sleepy old town that has largely escaped the tourist industry. The modern harbour is near the town, but a few kilometres to the north is a much more interesting ancient harbour. The old port of Al Qasir, called **Al Qasir Al Qadim**, had been a thriving port since pharaonic times, when it was known as Thagho. It may have been from here that the expedition to the Land of Punt set sail during the reign of Queen Hatshepsut, as inscribed on her funerary temple on the West Bank at Luxor.

The port prospered through Roman and Islamic times by being at the end of Wadi Hammamat, the most important route linking to the Nile at Coptos (modern Qift), taking five days. 'Myos Hormos' was described by Pliny the Elder and other Roman historians as one of the greatest Ptolemaic Red Sea ports, but its location has puzzled experts for years. It

Excavated amphora from Al Qasir's old port

Al Qasir seafront at dusk

was often thought to be at Abu Sha'r (near modern Al Gunah), controlling the entrance to the Gulf of Suez (and is still identified in that location on some maps). But researchers from the University of Southampton have recently uncovered evidence that the old port of Al Qasir Al Qadim and Myos Hormos are in fact one and the same. The later Ptolemies and Romans continued to use the same harbour, from which they exported wine, glass, pottery and textiles, whilst importing luxury goods such as spices, silk, pearls and medicines from India or even China. After the rise of Islam, Al Qasir maintained its status as the largest port in the Red Sea, used by pilgrims taking the route along Wadi Hammamat to Jeddah.

The old harbour entrance is now the beach of the Mövenpick Resort hotel, identified by a row of trees in a dip, just after the police checkpoint when entering Al Qasir from the north. All of the low-lying dark-brown silt on the land side was once the seabed of the old harbour. Excavations along the harbour have revealed the commercial and residential buildings of a thriving emporium. Private documents discovered in a 13th-century warehouse known as the **Sheikh's House** indicate a huge flow of trade through the port, and include the cargo list of a ship called 'Good Tidings', as well as zodiac charts, poetry and school texts.

Despite being the best natural harbour in the northern Red Sea, there were always problems supplying fresh water to Al Qasir. During the early 16th century the harbour appears to have irreversibly silted up. At the same time, the discovery of the sea route around Africa bypassed the Red Sea completely. The town expanded further south at this time, including the building of the **Ottoman Fort** (9am–5pm; charge) in 1571. The port formed the main link to the Holy Cities of Mecca and Medina on the other side of the Red Sea, also under Ottoman control. Excavations of the fort have revealed private letters from the 18th century relating to the provision of wheat from Upper Egypt, which regularly kept the Holy Cities alive. Many clay pipes were also found dating from the

## Wadi Hammamet

Evidence of trade along Wadi Hammamet from Al Qasir to the Nile goes back 6,000 years, with improvements about 3,000 years ago when a series of wells were dug during the New Kingdom period. The *wadi* has many beautiful rock carvings and hieroglyphic inscriptions. The ancient Egyptians mined gold at a place called Bir Umm Fawakhir halfway along the road. Other mines produced the green ornamental bekhen stone, which was also mined by the Romans, who guarded the route with watchtowers. Their ancient fire and smoke-signalling system protected pilgrims from Bedouin raids even into the 18th century. Closer to the Nile Valley are many *wadis* with unique inscriptions, but special permission is needed to visit these remote areas.

very earliest days of smoking tobacco almost 500 years ago.

The fort was rebuilt by the Napoleonic armies to withstand cannon fire, which it did for three days when the British warships HMS *Daedalus* and *Fox* demolished half the town in August 1799. When the French left in 1801 Mohammed Ali used the fort in his campaigns against the Wahabi sect in Hijaz on the other side of the Red Sea. The Egyptian army relinquished the fort in 1975, and it is now a good historical museum with Islamic, tribal and maritime sections, including a copy of Abraham Ortelius's Red Sea map from 1595, the original of which is now in the British Library.

Since the building of the Suez Canal, Al Qasir has lost most of its trade to Safajah, but some of its former glory can be seen between the fort and the modern seafront with its wonderful **Ottoman Red Sea Houses**. Most Red Sea

Old Ottoman houses in Al Qasir

ports (except Hodeida in Yemen and Jeddah in Saudi) have lost these wooden – and sometimes coral – houses, and these ones may not last much longer. Most are now abandoned and derelict and could soon be cleared away, but in the meantime you can enjoy wandering around the narrow lanes below the protruding painted wooden balconies.

Visiting Abdel Ghaffar's shrine

Around these streets are also many small mosques dedicated to the various holy men from places such as Morocco, West Africa, Somalia and India who have died here on pilgrimages. Immediately outside the Ottoman Fort is the **Shrine and Mosque of Abdel Ghaffar**, a Yemeni sheikh.

## MARSA' ALAM AND THE FAR SOUTH

The southernmost part of the coast is just starting to be discovered. Central to this development is the new Marsa' Alam international airport, actually 50km (30 miles) north of the town, which opened in 2006, with the majority of flights arriving from Italy. This far south almost all of the coastline has fringing reef only a few metres from the beach, so shore or beach diving is more popular here than relying on dive boats. Some European divers are put off by this, but many of the shore sites here are just as good as those you would have to get on an expensive boat to elsewhere.

## Marsa' Alam

**31** Strategically located just outside the airport is **Port Ghalib**, a large new development intended to rival Al Gunah in the north. This huge self-contained complex will ultimately have several resorts run by top-class hotel companies, a marina, golf course, shops and restaurants. Presently there are four hotels and a virtually empty marina with coffee shops and cafés. Check out its progress at www.portghalib.com.

Four km (2½ miles) south of this project is **Marsa Ombarak**, which served as a port at the end of Wadi Umbarak, another connecting route to the Nile. About 10km (6 miles) inland are the remains of an ancient goldmine at **'Om Rus**.

The town of **Marsa' Alam** itself is fairly nondescript, but important for fuel and buses if you are travelling under your own steam. Except for military vehicles, the main road is almost devoid of traffic, the mountains here are rugged and inhospitable and the sea is tranquil and inviting.

These southern resorts are very isolated with few outside

### There's Gold in Them Hills

King Tutankhamun's gold death mask was made from locally mined gold, but is there any gold left in the mines? The traditional notion that Egypt's gold was exhausted by the pharaohs, Romans and British – who worked many goldmines until the Suez Crisis – is currently being rethought. With gold at record prices, even small deposits are now economically viable.

A joint Egyptian-Australian mining company estimates over 55 million ounces remaining in the rich gold veins of the Red Sea hills, which today would total over US$50 billion, making it one of the largest goldfields in the world. The main open-cast site is at Sukari, about 25km (15 miles) up Wadi Al Jemal, a site known to have been exploited in ancient times and more recently by the British in the 1940s. The first ingot of modern Egyptian gold was poured in June 2009.

On the beach near Marsa' Alam

amenities, but they do have perfect beaches and local dive sites. **Marsa Abu Dabab**, 32km (20 miles) to the north of Marsa' Alam, has had a resident dugong (an endangered sea cow), which is an amazing sight underwater. For something completely different, nearby **Elphinstone Reef** is reachable in 20 minutes by rib from Marsa' Alam and is arguably one of the top five dive sites in the world and a must for shark-lovers.

## Wadi Al Jemal and the Alba National Park

**Wadi Al Jemal Protectorate** is 54km (33 miles) south of Marsa' Alam and is an ambitious project similar to the Nabeq Protectorate near Sharm El Sheikh. The coast and inland areas have been protected since 2003, but can be used by the local Ababda tribe under strict conditions. Sustainable trades, such as producing leather products for tourists, are encouraged. Offshore are mangrove swamps and Wadi Jemal Island, an important breeding site and haven for migrating birds, a nesting site for turtles and a habitat for dugongs. The protectorate is linked to the **Alba National Park**, a remote mountainous region with wild ostrich, Dorcas gazelle and Barbary sheep.

## Ras Banas Peninsula

Just north of the Ras Banas Peninsula, **Hamatah** is a some-what windswept community popular with kite- and wind-surfers and for dive boats going to remote dive sites. The most southerly resort in Egypt is **Lahami Bay**, just south of here, with an entire lagoon to itself, extensive 'house' reef diving and a fleet of dive boats for the more distant reefs.

Also to the north of the Ras Banas Peninsula is a diving area known as the **Fury Shoals**, a series of offshore reefs and over 30 dive sites, reached by day boats from some of the more southerly resorts. For more experienced divers, **Mikauwa Island** is a popular dive site located just off the tip of Ras Banas,

Turtles are regularly seen on the reefs

but it is only accessible from a 'liveaboard' dive boat, which can visit several dive sites in the area. Further out is **Zabargad Island**, the historic source of the semi-precious gem 'olivine' (a magnesium iron silicate) mined from 1500BC until the 20th century. Today the island is famous for its coral towers. Neighbouring **Rocky Island** has reef walls dropping well

Let's go diving!

over 1,000m (3,300ft) and is known for hammerhead and blacktail sharks, barracudas, manta and eagle rays, but experiences strong currents and frequent high seas.

## Berenice

Ancient **Berenice** is about 15km (9 miles) south of the small  village of **Arb Salh**, at a military checkpoint along the main road. The site was closed in 2004 for excavations and will re-open at some point in the future, but until then there is tight security everywhere. Strategically located just south of the large Ras Banas Peninsula that juts out 50km (30 miles) from the almost straight coastline, Berenice (locally Baraniss) was well protected from the strong north winds. Greek geographer Strabo mentions the bay, now called Foul Bay, during his travels. Offshore reefs and dangerous currents running around the peninsula have caused many shipwrecks, but these are currently out of bounds as the area is under military control.

Named after Berenice, the mother of Ptolemy II Philadelphus, the port was used from the 3rd century BC to the 6th century AD and developed mainly for importing African elephants to be used in wars against the Seleucids. Special

A camel trader in Shalatin

ships known as *elephantagoi* were used to transport the beasts after they had been captured further south along the Red Sea in what is now Sudan or Eritrea. They are also recorded in pictographs along the overland route through the Red Sea Mountains to Edfu on the Nile, with valuable emerald mines en route. Other carved scenes show camel caravans and the hunting of ibex and gazelle from the backs of camels. Other 'unofficial' routes through the mountains lack Roman or Greek evidence but were used by local Bedouin to avoid paying taxes. The time taken to get to Coptos (modern Qift) by the Roman route known as the Via Publica is said to have been 12 days.

The scope of later trade is shown in the items unearthed at Berenice from Java, South Asia and Persia. Documents in 11 languages dating from the Roman period (1st–4th centuries AD) have been found, as well as evidence of the worship of at least nine religious cults. Remains of the **Temple of Serapis**, excavated in 1818 by Belzoni, are also out of bounds.

Towards the end of Roman power, an inland nomadic group called the 'Blemmyes' became strong enough to attack the Roman port at Berenice, after which it was abandoned. The Blemmyes seem to have appeared in the 1st century AD and are most famous for being described as 'fantastic creatures' with their faces in the middle of their chests by the historian Pliny the Elder. They are probably the ancestors of the Beja tribe, nowadays found mainly along the Red Sea coast of Sudan.

## South to Shalatin

The **Tropic of Cancer** is crossed about halfway between Berenice and Shalatin, roughly where there is an area of protected mangroves at **Marsa Hamira**. The landscape is amazingly stark – a few Ababda huts are surrounded by dramatic mountains with huge rock walls and towering pinnacles.

**Shalatin** has a completely different feel to anywhere else in Egypt, and is more like sub-Saharan Africa. The Sudanese influence can be seen in the clothing, tatty market stalls and overloaded trucks ready to haul goods further south. This is still a sensitive region that Egypt disputes with Sudan, and the 'real' border is still another 170km (105 miles) away at Halayeb.

The main reason to come here is to visit the daily **camel market**. After arriving from Sudan the camels are held in quarantine pens, then they are bought and sold amongst hundreds of dealers, where an arbitrator oversees fair play.

Camel market

# WHAT TO DO

## SPORTS

### Scuba-Diving

The single most important reason why tens of thousands of visitors come to the Red Sea is to see the closest coral reefs to Europe. The clear waters and amazing marine life have been attracting divers ever since Hans Haas and Jacques Cousteau made their first Red Sea underwater films in the 1950s. All the major resorts and hotels have dive centres for hiring scuba equipment to certified divers and run courses for those wishing to qualify.

Operators based in Sharm El Sheikh include: **Red Sea College** (Naama Bay, tel: 069-360 0145, www.redseacollege. com), **Shark's Bay Diving** (Umbi Diving Village, Shark's Bay, tel: 069-360 0942, www.sharksbay.com) and **Sinai Divers** (Ghazala Hotel, Naama Bay, tel: 069-360 0150, www.sinai divers.com). At Dahab, **Fantasea Red Sea** (Coral Coast Hotel, tel: 069-364 1195, www.fantasearedsea.com). At Hurghadah, **Diving World** (beside Old Sheraton Hotel, Sakala, tel: 065-344 3582, www.divingworldredsea.com) and **Emperor Divers** (tourist harbour, Al Mina, tel: 065-345 0537, www.emperordivers.com). At Safajah, **Nemo Dive** (Maglis Madina, Corniche Street, tel: 065-325 6555, www. nemodive.com); at three locations around Marsa' Alam, **Red Sea Diving Safari** (tel: 02-3337 1833, www.redsea-diving safari.com); and at Lahami Bay, **Barakuda Diving** (Lahami Bay Hotel, tel: 012-224 2527; www.barakuda-diving.com).

World-class dive sites are all along the coast, with the main interests split between the numerous wrecks, large pelagic

Diving conditions in the Red Sea are excellent

fish, and the range of corals with smaller reef fishes. Each dive site is very specific in what it offers, with visibility, currents and types of large fish changing throughout the seasons. The only way to see a sunken ship in detail is to get a qualification and join the many divers exploring the famous wrecks such as the World War II *Thistlegorm* from Sharm El Sheikh or Hurghadah, and the *Salem Express* off Safajah. There is always the option of joining a 'liveaboard' for a few days, to reach the more remote reefs and wrecks that tend to be in a more pristine condition.

## Snorkelling

Snorkellers see the same beautiful colours of soft and hard corals and countless reef fish closer to the surface. Many

### World-Famous Dive Sites

The Egyptian Red Sea features in lists of the world's top dive sites – here are some of the most popular:

**Thistlegorm.** One the most famous wreck dives in the world, on a World War II freighter, still loaded with trucks, motorbikes and railway engines (see page 33).

**Abu Nuhas Islands.** At least four major ships have wrecked themselves on this reef over the past 150 years, including the P&O ship *Carnatic* and the Greek freighter *Giannis D*.

**Gordon and Jackson reefs.** Two of the string of dangerous reefs between Sharm El Sheikh and Tiran Island (see page 33), famous for large pelagic fish, particularly hammerhead and whale sharks.

**Elphinstone Reef.** Off Marsa' Alam, well known for excellent visibility and lots of sharks (see page 79).

**The Blue Hole.** North of Dahab, an unusual large hole running vertically through the coral reef (see page 41). Can be dangerous, as it is over 100m (330ft) deep.

Exploring the site at Thistlegorm

places sell or rent snorkel, mask and fins, and there are numerous safe bays in which to practise using the equipment. Snorkellers should be aware of the designated areas in which they are free to roam, away from the dangers of boats and other water-sport activities. Daily boat trips take snorkellers to secluded reefs and marine parks such as Ras Muhammad to see the pristine coral formations and reef fish.

## Glass-Bottomed Boat and Submarine Tours

There are several ways to see the wonders of the reef without even getting wet, let alone hiring loads of equipment and becoming a qualified diver. The simplest way is on board a glass-bottomed boat that slowly drifts across the top of the reef, allowing you to see the wonderful coral and fish. Many operators offer these tours from the beaches.

Larger boats go further out to more colourful reefs. Once in place, the viewer climbs down into an underwater section

Young windsurfer in Dahab

from which you can look horizontally at the reef wall as it slowly passes by. Divers often accompany these boats and feed the fish in front of viewers. **Seascope** semi-submarine operates at Hurghadah and Safajah (same tel: 065-344 7974), Port Ghalib (tel: 012-633 8865), Sharm El Sheikh (tel: 069-366 1393) and Taba (tel: 069-353 0560).

The **Sindbad** submarine is a fully submersible vessel descending to 25m (80ft) and the only recreational submarine in Africa. It is based at the Sindbad Club Resort, Hurghadah, although bookings arranged through many other hotels (tel: 065-344 9601, www.sindbad-club.com).

## Other Water Sports

Every conceivable water sport is available, from windsurfing, kitesurfing and wakeboarding to parasailing, water-skiing and banana rides, which are organised virtually on the spot. Certain places are ideal locations for different sports:

for windsurfing and kitesurfing try the permanently windy conditions of Ras Sudr in the Gulf of Suez; windsurfing is also very popular at Safajah.

Operators include **Colona Watersports**, at the Regency Plaza Hotel, Nabeq and Magawish Resort, Hurghadah (tel: 010-344 1810, www.colonawatersports.com), which offers many different water sports, including instruction courses in kitesurfing and wakeboarding.

## Desert Safaris

One of the most popular half- or full-day excursions is to travel into the desert to meet the local Bedouin. Transport can be any combination of camel, horse, jeep and quad bike, ending at a Bedouin tent for tea, *sheesha* pipe, barbecue and an evening's star-watching from the blackness of the desert. A small number of local eco-operators are committed to raising awareness of tribal ways of life, now under threat as many Bedouin are leaving the desert to work along the coast, attracted by the modern lifestyle on offer.

**Embah Safaris** (tel: 069-364 1690, www.embah.com), based in Dahab, run informative 4x4 safaris led by local Bedouin tribesmen lasting from one to seven days, exploring the hidden history and natural beauty of Sinai's stunning interior. **Red Sea Desert Adventures** (tel: 02-3337 1833; www.redseadesertadventures.com), based in Shagra Village near Marsa' Alam, offer safaris into the mountains to visit the ancient inscriptions and sites, lasting from one to several

Ready for a quad-bike safari

Camel trekking in Al Qasir

days and using local Bedouin leaders from the Ababda tribe as guides.

## Camel and Horse Riding

Riding a horse or camel across the desert or through the coastal surf is a great thrill. Early morning and late afternoon are the best times for avoiding the heat. Stables and riding schools are located at some of the larger resort hotels, such as the **Sofitel Equestrian Centre**, overlooking Naama Bay at Sharm El Sheikh (tel: 069-360 0081). At Al Gunah arrange camel and horse rides at the **Mövenpick Resort** or through the Swiss-managed **Yalla Horse Stables** near Abu Tig marina (tel: 065-354 9702/010-136 6703, www.elgouna.com). Horses and camels are also available along all the main beaches for shorter beach or desert rides.

## Golf

Despite the problems of water supplies, some amazing golf courses have been designed to professional standards, often utilising local grasses that require less water. Continual sunshine, low green fees and a relaxed atmosphere have all added to golf's popularity at upmarket resorts.

There is an 18-hole championship course at **Jolie Ville Golf**, Maritim Jolie Ville Resort, Coral Bay, Sharm El Sheikh (tel: 069-360 0635, email: info@sgr-maritim-jolieville.com); an 18-hole USPGA championship course at **Al Gunah** (tel: 012-746 4712, download a golf-course map and factsheet at www.elgouna.com); a 6,500m (7,100-yard) 18-hole course, beautifully situated between the Sinai Mountains and the Gulf of Aqaba at **Taba Heights** (tel: 069-358 0073, download a golf-course factsheet at www.tabaheights.com); and **The Cascades** (tel: 065-354 9896, www.somabay.com) at Soma Bay, with an 18-hole championship course and a 9-hole par-3 challenge course, both of which were designed by Gary Player.

## Other Activities

**Birdwatching.** Spring and autumn are particularly good times to observe birds migrating between their wintering in Africa and summer breeding areas in Europe and Asia. Cranes, storks, flamingos, bee-eaters and falcons are to be seen along this natural corridor using the Red Sea coast to navigate. Visit www.osme.org for further details of species that can be seen in the area.

**Camel racing.** The only real spectator sport in the region is seasonal camel racing; the largest event is in May at Sharm El Sheikh.

Go-kart racing in Sharm El Sheikh

**Go-karting.** One of the area's latest crazes is to hurtle around a track full of twists and turns in a small go-kart. Sharm El Sheikh has three circuits, of which the largest is the Ghibli Raceway (tel: 069-360 3939, www.ghibliraceway.com), built to profes-

sional FIA standards, next to the Hyatt Regency to the east of Naama Bay.

**Health clubs and gyms.** All large resort hotels have their own fitness centres for residents, as well as a choice of pools and saunas, some with wellness spas and natural treatment centres. The popularity of health centres for yoga, meditation and holistic treatment is particularly noticeable along the Gulf of Aqaba coast, from Dahab northwards.

**Ten-pin bowling.** The MAS Bowling Centre (tel: 069-360 2220) at Naama Bay and Soho Bowling at Soho Square both offer six bowling lanes. There is a five-lane bowling alley with pool tables at the Sindbad Club (tel: 065-344 9601, www.sindbad-club.com) in Hurghadah.

# ENTERTAINMENT

Hurghadah and Sharm El Sheikh both have a vibrant nightlife that will satisfy even the most active clubbers. For the less active there are plenty of live-music venues, casinos and belly-dancing shows. All resort hotels have extensive daily activity and nightly entertainment programmes. Check listings at hotels or in free local magazines and websites.

**Live music.** Several clubs, pubs and bars have live music at least one night a week, mainly rock and pop.

In Hurghadah, Papas Bar (tel: 012-329 7530) on Hurghada Marina Boulevard, and Papas II, next to the Shedwan Hotel in Ed-Dahar, both have karaoke, live bands and sports TV. PJ's Irish Bar (tel: 016-461 2045), next to the Roma Hotel in Sakala, is a lively venue.

In Sharm El Sheikh the Camel Bar and Roof (tel: 069-360 0700, www.cameldive.com) on King of Bahrain Street in Naama pumps out rock and dance music, with some live gigs on Thursdays, plus a chill-out space on the roof terrace. Tavern 2 (T2, tel: 012-778 5509), on the terrace of the aptly named Rock Hotel in Hadaba, regularly hosts live bands and has good DJ nights on Fridays. The original Tavern Bar is near the Camel Bar in Naama.

In Dahab, Rush, just south of the bridge, has live music on Wednesdays and stays open until 2am.

**Nightclubs.** An increasing number of world-class nightclubs are attracting a younger crowd to Egypt's main Red Sea resorts. Ministry of Sound, Hedkandi and Little Buddha recreate an Ibiza-style party atmosphere in both Hurghadah and Sharm. There are theme nights, such as Old Skool, house, celebrity DJs and foam parties, nightly until 4am. Full-moon parties are also a good excuse to dance the night away.

In Hurghadah, the Ministry of Sound (tel: 012-329 7530, www.ministryofsound.com) at Papas Beach Club in Sakala has top DJs and lively theme parties every night. Hedkandi Beach Bar (tel: 012-738 2442, www.hedkandibeachbar.com),

A DJ at the Little Buddha club

is now located in the Hurghadah Marina Boulevard, plays laid-back beach grooves.

In Sharm El Sheikh, Pacha Club (tel: 069-360 0197, www.pachasharm.com) on King of Bahrain Street in Naama is open until 4am, with theme nights and Ministry of Sound parties at weekends. The Little Buddha Sushi Bar and Lounge (tel: 069-360 1030, www.littlebuddha-sharm.com), with an imposing location in the middle of Naama Bay, stages Ibiza-style electro raves. New at Soho Square is the Pangaea Night Club (tel: 010-160 9544, www.soho-sharm.com).

**Casinos.** Hurghadah and Sharm El Sheikh both have several casinos. Blackjack and roulette are the most popular games, using chips bought with hard currency.

**Belly dancing.** Regular Elf Layla wa Layla (1,001 Nights) shows at Hurghadah (tel: 065-346 4603) and Hadaba in Sharm El Sheikh (tel: 069-366 4280).

## SHOPPING

Egyptians are expert salesmen with a great deal of charm and hospitality. Even if you're 'just looking', you'll be of-

Beads for sale

fered the chance to sit down and rest, have a tea or coffee and a friendly conversation in whatever language you choose – from Russian to Geordie. It is forbidden to buy or accept any items that come from the sea, including seashells, coral or shark's teeth, with heavy fines imposed at the airport.

**Gold and silver.** Specialist shops sell good-quality gold, silver and semi-precious gem-stones, mostly from Egypt, at reasonable prices compared to Europe. Marine and sea-life motifs are popular. Try Al Tawab Jewellery Group, with three outlets in Hurghadah – in front of Empire Hotel (tel: 065-354 6732) in Ad Dahar, at the Sindbad Club and at Jasmin Village; also try the Mövenpick Resort (tel: 065-333 2100) in Al Qasir.

**Rugs, carpets and cotton.** Carpet quality is very variable, but cheaper local rugs and mats are usually good value. Natural colours are beige, brown and cream, whilst more vibrant ones are dyed. Along the resort seafronts you can often find Bedouin women selling desert goods, such as camel belts and bags, usually made out of camel and goat hair or leather. The quality of Egyptian cotton is well known, so any local cotton item is often good quality and great value,

## Bargaining

Even if it is not in your nature to haggle over prices, it is all part of the buying process in Egypt. As a rule, try to settle for about half the initial price, or get something else thrown in for free. Try to take haggling less seriously and it can be great fun.

even if only a white T-shirt or *keffiyeh* headscarf. The long male *galabeya* dress is sometimes favoured by Westerners as a nightshirt. For local handicrafts and clothing try ISIS, Lay-

Coloured sand souvenirs

alena Hotel (45 Naama Center, tel: 065-360 2545) in Sharm El Sheikh.

**Spices and perfumes.** One of the most colourful sections of any local market is the spice section, where packets of good-quality spices do a brisk trade. Cumin, coriander, pepper and *shatta* (ground chillies and hot peppers) are all good for the kitchen at a fraction of prices back home. Many famous perfumes originate in Egypt. Today the art of the perfumier is less popular than it was 20 years ago, but Egyptian perfume is still good value if you know what you're looking for.

**Books and prints.** Tourist shops sell the usual locally produced photo books about the Red Sea and Sinai, but there aren't many specialist shops. In the backstreets of Old Sharm is a small bookshop belonging to the publishers Al Ahram which stocks some interesting books about the history, geology and wildlife of the Sinai, as well as informative divers' guides and maps.

If your interest in ancient Egypt has been stimulated, then there are some shops that sell copies and reprints of David Roberts's well-known 19th century Nile scenes, as well as some of his less famous views, such as St Catherine's Monastery or the Gulf of Aqaba.

**Papyrus.** Every tourist shop has reams of papyri of every possible size depicting all kinds of tomb scenes. These make great, uniquely Egyptian souvenirs, especially if you've visited Luxor, Aswan or Cairo.

## CHILDREN'S RED SEA

Egyptians are very family-orientated, and children are given a warm welcome across the country. There are several activities aimed specifically at children in the main resorts.

In such a hot and sunny climate, water parks are extremely popular, featuring a maze of snaking pipes and tubes, plunging into numerous pools. In Sharm El Sheikh, the massive **Aqua Park** (Ras 'Om Sid, tel: 069-366 5993, www.pickalbatros.com/aqua; daily 10am–sunset; charge) has 20 water slides, ranging from mini-slides for toddlers up to high-speed twisters for thrill-seeking teens. **Cleo Park** (Naama Bay, tel: 069-360 4400, http://cleopark.net; daily 10am–sunset; charge) has a similar collection of slides with a pharaonic theme. In the south of Hurghadah, **Sindbad Aqua Park** (Sindbad Club Resort, tel: 065-344 9601,

Aqua Park

www.sindbad-club.com; daily 10am–sunset; charge) offers more family fun.

**Fun Town** (tel: 069-360 2556; daily 4pm–midnight; charge) on Peace Road, near to the centre of Naama Bay in Sharm El Sheikh, has gentle rides for young children.

The **Sharm Museum** (Sharm Panorama, Naama Bay, tel: 069-360 0605, 012-739 0664, email: sharm_museum@ yahoo.com; daily 10am–2pm, 5pm-midnight; charge) is an easy way to get the children interested in ancient Egypt, with exact replicas of the famous statues found in the tombs of the pharaohs, particularly the boy-king Tutankhamun.

The **Red Sea Aquarium** (6 Corniche Street, Ad Dahar, Hurghadah, tel: 065-354 8557; daily 9am–10pm, closed Fri for prayers; charge) offers an insight into the area's rich marine life and an opportunity to observe the many types of fish close up, including sharks, turtles and stonefish.

**Dolphinella** (tel: 069-366 4855, 069-366 4866; daily; charge), opposite the Aida Hotel in Hadaba, Sharm El Sheikh, is to be enjoyed or avoided depending on what you think about keeping dolphins in captivity. Regular dolphin performance shows and the opportunity to swim with them at certain times. Similar is the newer Dolphin World Egypt (tel: 065-346 2740, www.dolphinworld-egypt.com) at Makadi, south of Hurghadah.

Tropical fish and coral

Children enjoy the excitement of a **horse or camel ride** out into the desert, as well as the chance to stop at a Bedouin tent for tea. Desert tours can be arranged through your hotel or local tour operators.

# Calendar of Events

**January** *Everywhere:* 7 January, Coptic Christmas. 19 January, Coptic Epiphany.

**February** *Al Gunah and Hurghadah:* international fishing competition run by the Egyptian Angling Federation (www.egaf.org).

**April** *Sharm El Sheikh:* International Sinai Bowling Championship organised by the Egyptian Bowling Federation, attracting ten-pin bowlers from around the world.

**May** *Sharm El Sheikh:* South Sinai Camel Festival, a tribal gathering for camel races of up to 15km (10 miles) at the racetrack close to the airport. Also includes other events such as archery, cross-country running and beach volleyball.

**June** *Sharm El Sheikh:* underwater photography contest. Entrants have limited digital memory and underwater time.

**July** *Sharm El Sheikh and Hurghadah:* national fishing competitions. *Hurghadah:* Oscar International Video Clip Festival (www.oscarvideoclip. com), a competition for the best music videos. *Soma Bay:* Red Sea Open Amateur Golf Championships.

**July–August** *Hurghadah:* tourism and shopping festival.

**November** *Sharm El Sheikh:* AVEX International Air Show (www.avex airshow.com), the largest business aviation show in the Middle East with aerial and static displays. *Sharm El Sheikh:* Sharmarathon – an international half marathon run at Ras Muhammad National Park. *Marsa Shagra:* 'Shark School' (www.redsea-divingsafari.com), workshops and dives exploring shark behaviour with an expert.

## Festivals fixed by the Islamic calendar:

**Ashura:** celebration of the martyrdom of Imam Hussein on the 10th of the Islamic month of Muharram.

**Moulid Al Nabi:** celebrates the birthday of the Prophet Mohammed.

**Eid Al Fitr:** festival at the end of Islamic fasting month of Ramadan.

**Eid Al Adha:** festival to mark Abraham's sacrifice.

Please check exact dates as they change year by year.

# EATING OUT

Being at the crossroads of Africa, Asia and the Middle East, the Egyptian Red Sea area offers a great variety of local and international dishes to suit all tastes. Historical influences over thousands of years have produced menus that are a delicious combination of Arabian, Indian, Persian, African, Turkish, Lebanese, Greek, Italian, and French flavours. From the most expensive meal at a top resort to street food enjoyed with the locals, the ingredients are generally fresh and often locally produced, with the speciality obviously being fresh fish and seafood.

The top chefs employed in the high-quality restaurants of the large resort hotels enjoy good reputations, preparing a wide range of international dishes in a variety of styles, with prices to match. Most other restaurants in the Red Sea towns are locally run and are therefore good places to try Egyptian food at reasonable prices. The innovative 'Dine Around' programme at Taba Heights allows guests to sample a variety of cuisines at other hotel restaurants.

## Favourite fuuls

Made from broad fava beans, *fuul* comes in a wide variety of popular dishes. Fuul Medammes is seasoned with cumin, olive oil, lemon and spices. Other combinations are with tomatoes, onions and peppers. Fuul Mubarak is a creamy sauce-and-egg mixture.

## WHEN TO EAT

When it comes to eating out, the pace of life in Egypt's Red Sea towns is similar to that in the southern Mediterranean. In the local towns breakfast can be taken at almost any time, with some cafés serving dishes from 6am to midday. Lunch is generally quite late, any time from 2pm to 5pm,

Beachside dining in a laid-back resort

and often the precursor to a light nap. The evening meal might not begin until 10pm and can stretch way beyond midnight. Resort hotels are mindful that many tourists prefer to eat earlier and serve food between set times accordingly.

## WHAT TO EAT

### Breakfast

In the mornings, one of the best local breakfasts (even provided in some resorts as part of their buffet) is a plate of steaming *fuul* – brown beans ladled from giant silver cooking pots called *idras*. With a few discs of local bread and steaming hot cups of sweet tea, this is great way to get the day moving, especially if it has lots of spices, peppers and tomato mixed in. Bread is the basic food for most of the population and can be found in many shapes and sizes, but mainly as a type of pitta bread. Large hotels offer vast break-

*Shawarma* seller in Old Sharm

fast menus, whereas smaller hotels are limited to more simple bread, cheese, omelettes, jam, tea and instant coffee, in
which case it might be worth stepping outside for an occasional local breakfast.

## Snacks and Street Food

Throughout the day there are delicious snacks to be bought,
but you will need to get away from the tourist restaurants
and into the local parts of town to find them. The popular
*felafel* sandwich is a great option for vegetarians, made from
deep- fried patties of mashed *fuul* beans and parsley, placed
into an envelope of local bread with finely chopped mixed
salad, *tahina* sauce *(see page 102)* and sometimes a pickle or
salad. Pickled vegetables are a great local favourite, a selection of which is called *torshi*.

   Giant vertical skewers of grilled lamb meat – 'doner
kebabs', also known as *shawarma* – are now commonplace

along the local streets and make a filling 'fast food' to be eaten on the move. Some local eateries advertise their golden grilled chickens in rotisseries placed out on the pavements and are usually cheerful places for a quick meal. A delicious sandwich is the cooked street food of *kibda*, small pieces of grilled liver placed inside a cut stick of bread, to which onions, chillies and spices are added (if you want it really hot, ask for extra crushed chilli powder, called *shatta*).

Care should be taken when eating street food, as some of the outlets might not be very hygienic and the food not very hot, which can cause stomach problems. However, this is not just a danger of locally prepared food, as some resorts and hotels cause a range of tummy problems by having under-

## Ramadan

The fasting month of Ramadan throws the whole process of mealtimes into disarray. The majority of Egypt's population do not eat, drink or smoke through the hours of daylight, but non-Muslims are permitted to use restaurants and cafés, most of which remain open, especially in the main resorts. It is courteous to refrain from eating, drinking or smoking outside in the streets of the towns during daylight. Some beer, wine and spirits shops close for the entire month, and local bars might also shut, but as most Red Sea resorts cater primarily for non-Muslims you will probably not notice much difference staying close to your hotel. Resorts catering for Egyptians and Arabs along the Gulf of Suez will have stricter rules about when food and drinks are available.

During Ramadan in the local parts of the towns, it is interesting to see and even be invited to join one of the open-air sunset meals, known as *iftar*, which can become great social occasions. Eating, drinking and having fun carries right through the night until the early morning meal, known as *suhuur*, the final meal before fasting begins again at sunrise.

heated buffet food standing around too long.

## Local Specialities

Menus for lunch and dinner in restaurants tend to be quite similar, starting with a few plates of appetisers, which are quite substantial in themselves. *Tahina* is a thin paste made from ground sesame seeds with added olive oil and spices, whilst *babaganugh* is mashed aubergine with garlic, lemon juice and oil. *Hummus* is a dip made from chickpeas now popular around the world.

A delicious dish imported from along the North African coast is *shakshouka*, a blend of chopped lamb, tomatoes, onions, herbs and spices, topped with an egg – try it if you see it on the menu. These popular starters are often accompanied by small dishes of pickled vegetables.

Taking inspiration from abroad, local salads have progressed greatly from the drab fare on offer of a few years ago. There are now wonderful Caesar, Greek, tuna and green salads available, all prepared with high-quality local produce from the Nile

### Fatah feasts

Local Bedouin feasts such as weddings are celebrated by eating *fatah* – a large dish heaped with rice and topped by hunks of meat. Sitting on the floor, each person will scoop up pieces of rice and meat with their right hand and pop them into their mouth.

Delta. A local style of thick soup, known as *molokiya*, is like an oily spinach broth, sometimes with rice in it, eaten with bread.

Some of the main meals on offer are fairly familiar, such as grilled meats, kebabs, chicken and pasta dishes, but there are also some remarkably tasty local specialities, such as pigeon (called *hammem*). They are often stuffed with rice or grain after being raised in pigeon houses (there are some in Hurghadah). Pigeons and quails can also turn up inside another North African import – *tagine*, a stew consisting of rice with onions, potatoes and tomato on a bed of rice or couscous with the meat placed on top.

## Desserts

*Om Ali* (meaning the 'mother of Ali') is a truly delicious pudding, presented in a hot baking pot. It is made from milk, nuts, dried fruit, coconuts, cinnamon and cream, separated by layers of thin corn bread. Baklava is a light filo pastry snack stuffed with honey and nuts, whilst *kunafa* is similar but made with a more delicate shredded pastry. *Basboosa* is a semolina cake, dripping with syrup and lemon.

One of the great legacies of so much overseas involvement in Egypt is the large number of patisseries in the towns and resorts, and many of the sweet sticky pastries will be familiar from Greece, Turkey or Lebanon. The alternative to all these rich, sweet pastries is a range of locally grown fresh fruit, such as bananas and dates, depending upon the season.

Dates growing in the desert

## WHAT TO DRINK

Tea will be offered everywhere, invariably sweet, black and thick, or possibly with mint. Intervene beforehand if you want it without sugar or with milk, although this is not always possible. There are many new internationally branded coffee shops, serving a choice of beans in trendy styles, but in traditional local coffee shops, it will either be instant Nescafé or thick Arabic (Turkish) coffee. Many of the resorts have their own version of a local thatched beach teahouse, where a selection of local teas and coffee can be taken, usually with great views out to sea – an ideal place to relax towards the end of the day.

Wandering around the local markets of Hurghadah or Sharm you will see dried purplish-red leaves piled up in baskets. These are the hibiscus blossoms used to make the refreshing drink called *karkadeh*, served hot or cold and originally from Nubia in southern Egypt. A delightful way to quench a raging thirst is with a local fruit juice from

### Ancient Beer and Wine

We know that beer has been made in Egypt for thousands of years from evidence found in pharaonic tombs and on wall-paintings. It was often used as a form of payment to workers and usually made by women as an offshoot of the yeast bread-making process. The method was similar to today, but the beer was probably a thick, sweet and nutritious brew, with minimal alcohol content. If beer was for the common workers in ancient Egypt, then wine was for the elite, as mentioned by many Greek historians. Some Egyptian temples even had their own vineyards to produce wine that was offered to the gods, of which Hathor – the main deity worshipped at the temple of Sarabet Al Khadem in Western Sinai – seems to have been the main recipient.

one of the many colourful stands. The choice depends on what is in season, such as mango, watermelon, strawberry, banana, pineapple, orange and other citrus fruits.

Many restaurants outside of the resorts serve alcohol, but smaller local places might not. Locally produced Stella beer comes in a variety of strengths, and the quality has risen dramatically in the past few years. Recent additions to the local beer market include a weaker Sakara brand and

Hibiscus blossoms are used to make *karkadeh*

two Meister beers, of which Meister Max is the stronger. Many international beers are imported to meet the demand from tourists. Local wines have also increased in quality to become fairly acceptable – the Omar Khayyam red is a safer bet than the Cru des Ptolémées white. Other new additions are the Lebanese-supervised Obelisk red and white wines, some of which are produced at Al Gunah. Some top restaurants shun local beer and wine, offering only imports, but with a hefty price attached. Influenced by Greek ouzo and Lebanese *arak*, there are Egyptian spirits with similar aniseed flavours, to be taken neat or with ice and water, whereupon they turn milky white. Duty-free shops in the main centres sell all the main brands of spirits, but remember to take your passport along.

The communal smoking of a *sheesha* (or hubble-bubble water pipe) is common in many local restaurants, cafés and beach bars. The tobacco itself is usually thick and pungent,

often mixed with fruit flavours such as apple or molasses. This activity is not confined to old men, and it is quite common to see a group of youngsters of both sexes sharing a *sheesha* in one of the restaurants. A long drink and the slow pull of water-cooled smoke always helps the sun go down after a hard day of being a tourist.

*Sheesha pipes*

## MENU READER

| | | | |
|---|---|---|---|
| **ahwa** | coffee | **kibda** | liver |
| **ananas** | pineapple | **kufta** | meatballs |
| **aysh** | bread | **laban, haleeb** | milk |
| **bakhteerkh** | watermelon | **lakhma** | meat |
| **bassal** | onions | **makaruna** | pasta |
| **batatas** | potatoes | **melh** | salt |
| **beera** | beer | **moyya** | water |
| **beerd** | eggs | **nabeet** | wine |
| **berinjan** | aubergine | **ruz** | rice |
| **bidoon lakhma** | without meat | **salata** | salad |
| **burtogaan** | oranges | **samak** | fish |
| **fattoura** | the bill | **shai** | tea |
| **filfil** | pepper | **shampinyon** | mushrooms |
| **frakh** | chicken | **shokolata** | chocolate |
| **fuul** | beans | **shorba** | soup |
| **gambari** | prawns/ shrimps | **sukkar** | sugar |
| | | **tamatum** | tomatoes |
| **hummus** | chickpeas | **toofa** | apple |
| **jibda** | cheese | **zaytoon** | olives |
| **khall** | vinegar | **zubda** | butter |

# PLACES TO EAT

*We have used the following symbols to give an idea of the price for a three-course meal:*

$$$$ US$40 and above   $$ US$10–25
$$$ US$25–40   $ less than US$10

## SHARM EL SHEIKH

**Abou El Sid $$** *Naama Bay, tel: 069-360 3910, 012-406 1260.* Part of the atmospheric Cairo chain of restaurants done out in oriental décor. Very good local food to be taken either in an air-conditioned room or on the outdoor roof terrace. It is easy to find as it is above the Hard Rock Cafe.

**Al Dente $$** *At Novotel Beach, Naama Bay.* Great Italian food prepared by specialist chefs and eaten in the open air, just behind the beach. A wonderful place to relax in the shade and people-watch.

**Andrea's $–$$** *Naama Bay, tel: 069-360 0972.* It's part of another Cairo chain, but the Egyptian food, served alfresco, is pretty good. One of the many open-air restaurants along lively and noisy Sultan Qaboos Street.

**Café Picasso $** *City Council Street, beside the go-kart track, Hadaba, tel: 010-926 6913.* High-quality Western meals and snacks served in a relaxed atmosphere. A bit off the beaten track, but there's the choice of eating inside or out, and great Sunday roast lunch with a free camel ride included.

**Da Franco $$–$$$** *Ghazala Beach Hotel, tel: 069-360 0150.* On the pedestrianised walkway behind the beach in Naama Bay. Genuine Italian specialities with pizzas straight from the wood-fired clay-brick oven. Next door is **Kokai $$$**, where good-quality Chinese and Japanese food is cooked before your very eyes.

**El-Masrien $** *Old Sharm, tel: 069-366 2904.* A grilled chicken restaurant that attracts a loyal crowd of Westerners for simple Egyptian food in pleasant surroundings. Another branch has recently opened in Nabeq to cater for the resorts beyond the airport.

**Fayrouz $$$$$** *Ritz Carlton Hotel, Ras 'Om Sid, tel: 069-366 1919.* Luxurious setting for top quality Lebanese speciality cuisine. Colourful Oriental rugs, cushions, decor and terrace area, accompanied by discreet live local music and dancing. Menu has a vast choice of hot and cold mezzeh, followed by char-grilled seafood or meat. Large selection of fine wines from around the world. Evenings only 6.30pm–10.30pm, smart dress.

**Felfela $** *Old Sharm.* Wonderful local Egyptian dishes, based on those in the original Felfela restaurant in central Cairo. Everything is great value, tasty and a welcome change from Western-style food. Try *shakshouka* as a starter, quail for main (or one the many *fuul* dishes for vegetarians) and Om Ali as dessert.

**Hard Rock Cafe $$$** *Downtown Naama Bay, tel: 069-360 2664, www.hardrock.com.* You really can't miss the sky dome, huge guitar and pink 1950s car outside this extremely popular night spot. American food is served in this lively and noisy bar. Open noon–2am.

**Il Frantoio Italian Restaurant $$$$** *Four Seasons Hotel, Shark's Bay, tel: 069-360 3555.* An extremely elegant Italian restaurant with refined and inventive cooking, using only the best ingredients, where you can eat inside or alfresco. Try the home-made ravioli or grilled, stuffed sea bass. Ideal for that special occasion.

**Kanzaman $$** *El-Zhoor mall, opposite Cataract Hotel, Naama Bay, tel: 064-345 6899, 012-710 5877, www.kanzamanredsea. com.* On the corner of a street full of open-air restaurants where everyone wants your business. This place specialises in barbecue and seafood, whilst next door is the reputable **Fish Market** franchise, which has a deserved reputation from its Cairo restaurants.

**Silk Road $$$$** *Grand Rotana Resort and Spa, Shark's Bay, tel: 069-360 2700.* The hotel's signature restaurant with consistently high quality food in a choice of Arabian, Chinese, Thai and Indian styles, prepared by visiting Asian chefs. Dress smartly for a chic location. Evenings only from 7pm to 11pm. Reservations recommended.

**Red Sea Fish $$** *Old Sharm, tel: 069-366 4250, www.redseafish-sharm.com.* The gaudy exterior hides an award-winning restaurant specialising in locally caught fish and seafood.

**Tam Tam $$$** *Ghazala Hotel, Naama Bay; tel: 069-360 0150.* Excellent Egyptian and Middle Eastern speciality dishes served indoors in a very pleasant first-floor restaurant or outside on the terrace, both overlooking the beach.

**Zaza Panorama $** *Above Sharm Museum, Naama Bay, tel: 012-731 2972.* Pizzeria and wine bar built into the cliffs on a series of cushioned terraces with stunning views over Naama Bay. The perfect place to catch the breeze and enjoy a cool drink on a hot evening whilst the twinkling lights switch on around the bay.

## DAHAB

**Al Capone $$** *Beside the bridge, Asilah, tel: 010-372 2220.* Italian cuisine and fish come together at this busy central location along the corniche walkway. Eat indoors upstairs or choose the beachside location like everyone else.

**Arisha $** *Coral Coast Hotel, Asilah, tel: 069-364 1195.* Good food from the kitchens of the Coral Coast Hotel served in the wonderfully relaxed atmosphere of a thatched beachside bar. A long lunch here can easily turn into a lazy afternoon and evening.

**Funny Mummy $** *Al Mashraba.* Good-value food at a lively bar restaurant with great coastal views from the roof terrace, attracting a faithful clientele. Opposite is the Sphinx Bar, which livens up at night with loud music and free pool tables.

## TABA HEIGHTS

**Hyatt Regency, Intercontinental, Marriott, Sofitel, Three Corners, Sea Club and Uptown $$$–$$$$** *www.tabaheights. com.* Extend your choice of eating by joining the 'Dine Around' programme which allows you to eat at any of the seven locations in the Taba Heights complex regardless of your hotel of residence. Thai, Italian, Mexican, Indian, Middle Eastern and Lebanese restaurants can all be accessed by the free shuttle bus running around the resort.

## AL GUNAH

**Orient 1001 $$$** *Sheraton Miramar, tel: 065-354 5606, ext 110.* Good Lebanese dishes and Egyptian seafood in a wonderful oriental setting located on its own island. Live shows every Sunday and Thursday.

**Spagheteria del Porto $$$** *Abu Tig Marina, tel: 065-354 9702 ext 77963.* Well-prepared traditional Italian dishes, with fish and seafood as specialities. Make sure you save some space for one of the great desserts.

**White Elephant Thai Restaurant $$–$$$** *Kafr Al Gunah, tel: 065-345 9702, 010-102 5117.* Authentic, good-quality Thai cuisine whipped up by a Thai chef. One of the most popular choices for eating outside of your resort in El-Gouna.

## HURGHADAH (AL GHARDAQAH)

**Beduin $$$$** *Iberotel, Makadi Bay, tel: 069 359 0000.* Speciality grill of typical Egyptian, Middle Eastern and Oriental dishes served in Eastern setting. Only open for dinner 7pm to 9pm daily. Partakes in the Makadi Bay 'dine-around' programme.

**Café del Mar $–$$** *Sea Tower building, beside Al Arosa Square, Sakala, tel: 010-071 6770.* A simple no-nonsense café with generous portions of fresh food. Breakfasts, salads, sandwiches and grills.

**Da Nanni $$** *Hadaba Road (next to La Perla Hotel), Sakala, tel: 065-344 7018, 010-663 3162.* The Italian couple who run this *ristorante* serve classic Italian pasta and pizza in a cosy atmosphere. Open 5–11pm.

**El-Joker $$–$$$** *Midan Sakala, tel: 065-354 3146.* A very popular fish restaurant right in the centre of Sakala on the roundabout, serving simple but excellent fresh fish by weight, accompanied by bread and salads. No alcohol.

**Felfela $** *Sheraton Street, Sakala, tel: 065-344 2411.* Another branch of the popular Cairo chain, serving good-value tasty Egyptian food as usual. This place has a stunning coastal location to the south of Sakala, which alone is worth double the cost of the meal. A great place for a lazy relaxing meal, well away from the noise of Hurghadah.

**Fish House $$** *Sheraton Road, Sakala, tel: 065-344 1771, 010-160 7500.* Recommended fish restaurant on the first floor above the affiliated **Sushi House**. Easy to find as it is next door to McDonald's.

**Hard Rock Cafe $$$** *Nawarra Centre, Al Kora Street, tel: 065-346 5170, www.hardrock.com.* Part of new Hurghadah to the south, established in 2004. A popular night spot where American and TexMex food is served in a lively and noisy bar. Open noon–3am.

**Mandarine Lebanese $$$** *Corniche, Ad Dahar (in front of Shedwan Garden Hotel), tel: 065-354 7007.* Innovative Lebanese food served in an agreeable setting, part of the Shedwan Garden Hotel group. Along the same street are the related Gaucho Argentinian steak house, Mafia Italian café and Golden Dragon Chinese.

**Red Sea Reunion $$** *Hospital Street, Ad Dahar, tel: 012-719 6267, www.redseareunion.com.* Good food and alcohol served indoors or on the great open-air rooftop terrace of this Dutch/Egyptian eatery. Comfortable atmosphere with great service.

**Star Fish $$** *Sheraton Road (between Al Joker and Golden Sun Hotel), tel: 065-344 3750.* Tasty fish dishes in a variety of styles such as smoked herring layers and calamari with seafood and nuts. No alcohol.

**Sunset $** *Sayed Korrayem Street, Ad Dahar.* Popular Dutch-owned restaurant just down from the Triton Empire Hotel. Serves great- value freshly prepared pasta dishes and salads. An ideal place for people-watching along the seafront with a wine, beer or cocktail in the early evening before going elsewhere.

**White Elephant Thai Restaurant $$–$$$** *Hurghadah Marina, Sakala, tel: 010-102 5117.* A great selection of delicious spicy Thai food, especially the variety of fish dishes with ingredients obtained fresh from the nearby fish market at the harbour.

## AL QASIR

**El-Ferdos $** *Corniche (opposite police station), tel: 018-332 4884.* The air-conditioning is going full blast inside, but outside are pleasant tables on a quiet beach. Great for local grilled fish or seafood caught that day. No alcohol.

## MARSA SHAGRA

**Red Sea Diving Safari $$** *Marsa Shagra, 20km (12 miles) north of Marsa' Alam, tel: 02-3337 1833, 02-3337 9942, www.redseadivingsafari.com.* A wonderfully located terrace overlooking the sea where you can eat fresh fish and a fine array of local dishes.

## LAHAMI BAY

**Seven Seas $$$** *Lahami Bay Beach Resort, 115km (71 miles) south of Marsa' Alam, tel: 012-317 3344, 019-510 0354, www.lahamibay.com.* The fine selection of local fish and seafood can be eaten inside or out on a large terrace, overlooking the pool and distant tranquil lagoon.

# A–Z TRAVEL TIPS

A Summary of Practical Information

## A

**ACCOMMODATION** (see also CAMPING, YOUTH HOSTELS and list of RECOMMENDED HOTELS)

There are plenty of resort hotels in a wide range of locations stretching all the way along the coastline, with some specialising in activities such as diving, windsurfing or golf. Some are locally owned, whilst others belong to the top international chains.

The majority of tourists purchase packages with flights and hotels included, and this can often be much better value than buying flights and accommodation separately. Walk-in rates can be very expensive, so always try to book online in advance for the best deals.

There are a few small locally owned hotels in the older centre of Hurghadah, but not many in the Sharm El Sheikh area. Most hotels accept credit cards, but some of the smaller places will only accept US dollars, euros or British pounds as cash.

| hotel | **fondu** |
| how much? | **bi kam?** |

## AIRPORTS

The airports at Sharm El Sheikh, Hurghadah, Marsa Alam and Taba are modern and well organised. Exchange banks and visa purchases are located before immigration, with ATM bank machines often outside. Hotel transfers seldom take longer than 30 minutes, except to the most remote resorts from Marsa Alam and Taba.

## B

## BICYCLE HIRE

Along the seafronts of the main centres are a few shops that rent out bicycles, which can be a good way to get between the resorts and bays. The most pleasant routes are along pedestrianised coast roads at Dahab, Naama Bay, Nabeq and south Hurghadah, which avoid the danger of traffic. Be aware that most bicycles are not very well maintained and hired without helmets.

## BOAT HIRE

Dive boats are usually hired by the day on excursions run by dive centres and resorts, with the cost split by the divers. The cost is often included in the total diving fees. Boats can be hired privately from one day up to one month. Boats can also be hired for deep-sea fishing day trips. Note that fishing is not allowed anywhere off Sharm El Sheikh, and there is also a total ban on spear fishing in Egypt.

## BUDGETING FOR YOUR TRIP

Hurghadah, Sharm El Sheikh, Marsa' Alam and Taba all benefit from good-value charter flights from major European airports. Hotels can be expensive if not booked in advance or as part of a tour package. If you have one, bring an International Student Identification Card (ISIC) for discounts on entry fees, dive courses, internal air travel, and some accommodation and restaurants.

The following prices in LE (Egyptian Pounds) and US$ will give a rough idea of how much you can expect to spend:

**Airport transfer.** From Sharm El Sheikh or Hurghadah international airports to the centre of town US$30.

**Car hire.** From US$60 per day.

**Guides.** Trekking or desert guide for a half-day tour or to climb Mount Sinai US$30.

**Hotels.** Probably your largest expense at US$20–400 per night.

**Internet cafés.** 5–20LE per hour.

**Meals and drinks.** A set menu or buffet lunch/dinner in a two/three-star hotel or local restaurant 50–100LE, in a four/five-star hotel 150–250LE. Evening meal in a downtown restaurant 100–200LE. Soft drink/coffee in a café 5–10LE.

**Sightseeing.** Entry to a national park or other protected site 50LE.
**Taxis.** Short trip (3km/2 miles) within central Hurghadah or Sharm
El Sheikh 30LE, longer trip (10km/6 miles) from one end of a city
to the other 60LE.

## C

## CAMPING

There are a few official campsites with toilet and washing facilities
along the coast, such as at Ras Muhammad National Park, and a
number of beach resorts allow campers to pitch tents. Rough camping is not easy as many coastal areas are under military control.
Note that within Sinai there are still areas of landmines.

Overnight camping for groups organised by desert safari operators will be on private tribal land with access to cooking and washing facilities, usually in a local house or hut.

## CAR HIRE (See also DRIVING)

Although it is possible to hire a self-drive car or 4x4 and make your
way around the coast or desert, in reality this may prove extremely
complicated. Some attractions are very difficult to find, and others
(such as the Coloured Canyon near Nowibe) need special permission
from the tourist police, whose office also needs to be found. Off-road
trips involve the additional dangers of getting lost in the desert or
finding one of the many landmines still left over from the Israeli war.

Hiring a car with a driver for a day, week or month does not cost
much more and gives you a lot more flexibility. Most tourist sites
are accessible by public transport or taxis, and 4x4 adventures into
the Eastern Desert or Sinai can be easily arranged through a local
tour operator *(see pages 89 and 131)*.

If you do hire a car, make sure you have plenty of insurance, an
international driving permit and are at least 25 years of age. **Avis**
(www.avisworld.com) has offices in Hurghadah (outside Aqua Vil-

lage, Sheraton Road, tel: 065-344 7400) and Sharm El Sheikh (Morghana Trade Centre, Naama Bay, tel: 069-360 2400). There are also several local hire companies such as **CRC Rent-a-car & Limos** at 5/6 Al Bashira Centre (next to Grand Hotel), Hurghadah (tel: 010-610 7387, email: crc_hurghada@yahoo.com) and Plaza Mall, Naama Bay, Sharm El Sheikh (tel: 010-181 1035). Also in Sharm El Sheikh is the firm **SMG**, based at several hotels.

## CLIMATE

The Red Sea is in the middle of a desert region, and there are only two main seasons – mild winters and hot summers. Temperatures throughout the year average between 14°C (57°F) and 28°C (82°F), but can climb to over 40°C (104°F) in the summer months of June, July and August. It gets hotter the further south you go towards Sudan. In winter, winds can be cold in the desert, at sea or at altitude. Rainstorms are unusual, but can occur late winter. The following chart gives the average monthly temperatures in Sharm El Sheikh:

| | J | F | M | A | M | J | J | A | S | O | N | D |
|---|---|---|---|---|---|---|---|---|---|---|---|---|
| °C | 14 | 15 | 18 | 22 | 25 | 27 | 28 | 28 | 27 | 23 | 20 | 16 |
| °F | 57 | 59 | 64 | 71 | 77 | 82 | 84 | 84 | 82 | 73 | 68 | 60 |

## CLOTHING

Loose-fitting clothes made from natural fibres are the best all year round. Swimwear is acceptable on the beach and inside resort complexes, but topless sunbathing is illegal. Tourists should try to dress conservatively (ie no bikinis or swimwear) when visiting local areas such as Old Sharm or when travelling in minibuses or taxis, so as not to offend locals, particularly during the holy fasting month of Ramadan. Doing so will make the experience more enjoyable and ensure that women in particular receive much less hassle. Men and women wearing unsuitable clothing will be given a wraparound at sites such as St Catherine's Monastery. Bring a sunhat, high-factor sun cream and sunglasses. In winter a jacket is handy, and layers of clothing will help keep you warm in a cold wind. Bring comfortable walking shoes for the desert and other uneven or difficult terrain. Some top resorts have dress codes for their restaurants.

## CRIME AND SAFETY

The main concerns are petty theft and terrorist attacks. The vast majority of Egyptians are friendly and helpful people, but there is occasional pickpocketing or distraction theft. If anything is stolen, go immediately to a police station and obtain a report for insurance purposes. There are always plenty of Tourist Police around the main resorts to help if you have any difficulty (see POLICE).

Egypt has suffered some terrible terrorist attacks in the past decade, with bombings in the Sinai resorts of Taba, Sharm El Sheikh and Dahab. The authorities have set up security checks at all resorts, hotels, tourist sites and harbours. Tourists should avoid any local demonstrations that are part of the general uprisings following the 'revolution' in early 2011. Considering the sheer number of tourists visiting the Red Sea resorts every year, there are surprisingly few problems.

## D

## DRIVING (see also CAR HIRE)

If you intend to drive a car you will need your national licence, an international driving permit, and photocopies of your passport and visa. Take special care if hiring a 4x4, as driving off-road in the desert can be dangerous and you should be fully equipped. Observe directions from the police and military at the numerous checkpoints and heed warning signs about minefields. If driving a quad bike, scooter or motorbike, ensure that you have a correctly fitting helmet and insurance to cover the activity.

# E

## ELECTRICITY

Egypt uses 220v–240v/50Hz current, so most European appliances will work fine; US devices designed to use 110v will need a transformer. Most sockets take standard Continental European round two-pin plugs.

## EMBASSIES AND CONSULATES

The embassies are all in Cairo:

**Australia:** World Trade Centre 11th Floor, Corniche Al Nil, Bulak, Cairo, tel: 02-2570 2975, fax: 02-2570 2979.

**Canada:** 26 Kamel Al Shenawy Street, Garden City, Cairo, tel: 02-2794 3110, fax: 02-2796 3548, email: cairo@dfait-maeci.gc.ca.

**Ireland:** 3 Abu Al Feda Street, Zamalek, Cairo, tel: 02-2340 8264/8547, fax: 02-2341 2863.

**South Africa:** 21–23 Giza Street, 18th Floor, Giza.

**UK:** 7 Ahmed Ragheb Street, Garden City, Cairo, tel: 02-2794 0852/0/8, fax: 02-2794 3065, email: consular.cairo@fco.gov.uk, http://ukinegypt.fco.gov.uk/en. The consular section can be contacted by telephone on 02-2791 6000 Sun–Thur 9am–2pm, and is open for personal callers Sun–Thur 9.30am–1.30pm, except holidays.

**US:** 5 Latin America Street, Garden City, Cairo, tel: 02-2797 3300, fax: 02-2797-3200.

## EMERGENCIES

Report any emergency to the nearest Tourist Police, security officer or army personnel.

Emergency telephone numbers are:

Police: **122**

Tourist Police: **126**

Ambulance: **123**

Fire: **125**

## G

### GAY AND LESBIAN TRAVELLERS

Homosexuality is technically illegal in Egypt, but some couples do have same-sex relationships and certain nightclubs and bars are gay hangouts. Gay and lesbian visitors will encounter few problems as long as they are discreet and cautious about any outward signs of affection towards each other. Local men often greet other with kisses and hold hands, but this is not the sign of a gay relationship.

### GETTING THERE (see also TOURIST INFORMATION)

**By air.** Some major airlines, including EgyptAir, easyJet, Austrian Airways, Air Berlin and Royal Jordanian, fly to airports on the Red Sea, but tourist charter flights, usually on weekly departures, are more widely available from major European cities. The national carrier EgyptAir (www.egyptair.com.eg) links local airports to Cairo, Luxor, Aswan and Alexandria and flies to some European and US cities.

**By road.** The land border with Israel is at Taba. Be aware that even without an Israeli stamp in your passport, an Egyptian entry/exit stamp at this border will make your passport unusable in some other Arab countries, as this implies entry to or from Israel.

**By sea.** There are two ferries departing daily in the late morning from Aqaba in Jordan and sailing to Nowibe in Sinai (tel: 069-352 0427, 010-668 0260 in Nowibe). These can be very overcrowded.

### GUIDES AND TOURS

The short daily excursions and desert safaris advertised in the main tourist centres of Sharm El Sheikh and Hurghadah will be accompanied by a guide, but tour agencies can provide a 4x4 vehicle, driver and guide for any number of days, to visit desert sites, for trekking and camping in the Eastern Desert or Sinai, or for your own itinerary to the Nile Valley, Cairo, Luxor and Aswan. For details of expert desert safari tour operators, *see page 89*.

Recommended operators include:

**Highway Travel** (www.highwaytravel.travel), Hurghadah: Shorouk Al Hadaba building, Al Shamalia Road, tel: 012-743 4256, 065-344 4764; Sharm El Sheikh: Office 11, Mall #8, Naama Bay, tel: 012-743 4260, 069-360 2235; Taba: Sea Star Resort, tel: 012-743 4258, 069-353 0295.

**Seti First Travel** (www.setifirst.com), Hurghadah: front of Shedwan Village; Ad Dahar, tel: 065-354 8546; Sharm El Sheikh: Seti Palm Sharm Beach Resort, Sharm Al Maya, tel: 069-366 0870.

**Spring Tours** (www.springtours.com), Hurghadah: Village Road, tel: 065-344 0803, Sharm El Sheikh: Mall #8, Naama Bay, tel: 069-360 0131.

# H

## HEALTH AND MEDICAL CARE

Most tourist illnesses are temporary, seldom lasting more than 24 hours. Stomach upsets are the most common, often due to poor hygiene, unclean water or change of environment. Too much sun can also cause problems, so always wear a sunhat, sunglasses and use high-factor sun cream. Drink bottled water and avoid food that is not freshly cooked or has been lying around for a long time. Full health insurance is recommended.

**Vaccinations.** None are compulsory, but polio, tetanus, typhoid and hepatitis A are recommended. Check www.mdtravelhealth.com.

For less serious ailments, there are plenty of modern pharmacies where you can get quick, professional advice and medicines. Hotels can always call for an English-speaking doctor or locate an open pharmacy. There are very good hospitals in Hurghadah and Sharm El Sheikh, some of which accept credit cards, whilst others need to be paid in cash. Costs can then be reclaimed from your travel insurance.

**Sharm El Sheikh International Hospital**, Peace Road, Hai Al

Nour near Hadaba, tel: 069-366 0893.

**Al Ghardaqah International Hospital**, Al Ahya on road to Al Gunah, tel: 065-355 3439, 012-340 0291.

| | |
|---|---|
| Help me! | Il ha ooni! |
| call a doctor | ayzin doktor |

## HOLIDAYS

There are two types of official holidays when government offices and banks are closed, secular (fixed) and religious (variable dates). Islamic dates move forward roughly 11 days every year with the Islamic calendar. The fixed holidays are:

| | |
|---|---|
| 7 January | Coptic Christmas |
| 22 February | Union Day |
| 25 April | Sinai Liberation Day |
| 1 May | Labour Day |
| 18 June | Evacuation Day |
| 1 July | Bank Holiday |
| 23 July | Revolution Day |
| 11 September | Coptic New Year |
| 6 October | Armed Forces Day |
| 23 October | National Liberation Day |
| 24 October | Suez Victory Day |
| 23 December | Victory Day |

Egypt's variable holidays which change with the Islamic calendar are:

| | |
|---|---|
| *Fatih Muharram* | Islamic New Year |
| *Ashura Day* | commemorates the martyrdom of Hussein ibn Ali |
| *Eid Al Fitr* | (The Minor Feast) celebrates the end of Ramadan for three days |
| *Eid Al Adha* | (The Grand Feast) commemorates the sacrifice of Abraham |

# L

## LANGUAGE

Arabic is the official language, with Egyptian Arabic widely understood throughout other Arab countries through Egyptian television, cinema and music. Even a few words of Arabic will be appreciated by the locals. In these tourist resort many locals speak English.

Some useful Arabic words and phrases:

| | |
|---|---|
| yes/no | aywa/la |
| hello | salam aleykum |
| (response to hello) | aleykum salam |
| hello/welcome | ahlan wa sahlan |
| OK | tamam, maashi |
| please | min fadlak |
| thank you | shukran |
| (response to thank you) | afwan |
| how are you? | izayak? |
| I am fine | al humdillilah |
| good morning | sabah al-kher |
| good evening | mesa al-kher |
| goodbye | ma'a salama |
| what is your name? | izmak eh? |
| my name is... | izmi... |
| I do not understand | ana mush fahem |
| do you speak English? | inta bititkalem inglizi? |
| market | souq |
| mosque | jama |
| town | medina |
| right | yammen |
| left | shemal |
| straight ahead | allatool |

# M

## MAPS

Reasonable maps of the Red Sea (but only as part of Egypt) are available outside of the country. The most detailed is Kümmerley and Frey *Egypt* 1:950,000, also available in some souvenir and bookshops in Egypt printed by Lehnert and Landrock. The Insight FlexiMap of Egypt is 1:930,000 scale, double-sided and laminated to prevent ripping.

Sinai is better covered, with the most detailed map being the excellent but hard-to-obtain 1994 *South Sinai – Map of Attractions* 1:250,000 Survey of Israel published by Tzofit Ltd. Also try the Reise Know-How Verlag *Sinai* 1:500,000, which is available in the UK from Stanfords in London (www.stanfords.co.uk). Another local Lehnert and Landrock map is the Kümmerley and Frey *Sinai* 1:850,000.

There are several Hurghadah and Sharm El Sheikh maps available free from hotels and tour operators, but these are often overloaded with adverts and have confusing scales and graphics.

## MEDIA

**Newspapers.** *The Egyptian Gazette* (www.egyptiangazette.net.eg), established in 1880, is published daily and is sometimes on sale in Hurghadah. Published every Thursday is *Al-Ahram Weekly* (http://weekly.ahram.org.eg), an English-language version of the respected state-owned Arabic newspaper *Al-Ahram*.

Locally published and with interesting articles about the Hurghadah region is the free bimonthly *Red Sea Bulletin* (www.redseapages.com). The bimonthly diving magazine *h2o* is also free (www.h2o-mag.com). There are two versions of the pocket-sized *Hello Red Sea*, one for Hurghadah area, another for Sharm El Sheikh. Sharm has a few free magazines such as *Sharm Guide*, *Mix*, *Sharm in My Pocket* and *The Book* (www.thebook-sharm.com). *The Peninsula* appears irregularly and costs US$3.

**TV and radio.** Television Channels 1 and 2 are national, with English news nightly on Channel 2. Channel 3 is the Cairo channel, with Nile TV and Dream TV providing some imported English programmes. Most hotels have satellite and cable TV, offering greater choice from overseas. On the radio is the BBC World Service, and English news can be found at FM95. The first private radio station in Egypt, Al Gunah Radio, can be heard in Al Gunah and Hurghadah on 100.0FM.

## MONEY

The Egyptian pound (LE) is tied to the US dollar. There are Egyptian currency notes for 100, 50, 20, 10, 5, 1 LE, 50 and 25 piastres (100 piastres = 1LE). There are new 1LE coins.

Most of the local economy operates on cash, and outside of the hotels you should do the same. Cash can be obtained on a debit/credit card from one of the many ATMs, otherwise you can exchange US dollars, euros or British pounds at money exchanges. When exchanging money, insist on small denominations as nobody has any change.

## O

## OPENING TIMES

**Banks.** 8.30am to 2pm, closed Friday, Saturday and most holidays.
**Business.** 8am to 4 or 5pm, closed Friday, some closed Saturday, and most holidays.
**Government offices.** 8am to 3pm, closed Friday and most holidays.
**Shops.** Daily 9am to 10pm in summer (10am to 9pm in winter).

## P

## PHOTOGRAPHY

Egypt can be a photographer's dream, with so much colour and vibrant local life. Take as much memory as you need, as compatible local supplies are uncertain. Ask before taking photos of people, and respect their wishes. Underwater photography equipment can be hired as part of your diving gear, with photos then downloaded onto a disc for you.

## POLICE

There is a bewildering assortment of uniformed guards, police and army personnel on duty, mainly for your safety. Tourists in need of help will usually be quickly attended to by an English-speaking officer. Tourist Police are generally helpful, especially those working in offices at the airports. Reporting a crime or theft can be time- consuming due to the paperwork involved.

## POST OFFICES

The postal system generally works very well. Stamps can be bought from hotels, post offices and some shops. Most post offices are painted green and open every day, except Friday and some holidays, from 8.30am to 3pm. Allow five days for airmail to Europe and up to two weeks to the US.

## PUBLIC TRANSPORT

**Taxis.** The best way to get around the resorts is in an official taxi. Always fix a price before getting in by asking local advice on how much the fare should be. If you find a good taxi driver who speaks some English, pay them to wait for you, or maybe hire them for a few hours.

**Buses.** Daily buses run between the main towns along the coast, and to Suez and Cairo, usually with courtesy stops every two hours or so. In Sinai most services are run by East Delta Travel (tel: 069-366 0600), connecting Suez, At Tur, Sharm El Sheikh, Dahab, Nowibe and Taba. Upper Egypt Travel, Al Gunah and Super Jet operate services south of Suez to Hurghadah, Safajah, Al Qasir and Marsa' Alam. Local buses also run to the Nile Valley from the coast, but tourists are not usually permitted to use these for security reasons.

**Minibuses.** This economical way of getting from one suburb to another is used mainly by Egyptians. Minibuses only run along set routes such as Peace Road around Sharm El Sheikh.

**Ferries.** This should be the ideal way to get between the two main centres of Hurghadah (tel: 065-344 9481) and Sharm El Sheikh (tel: 069-360 0936, 012-822 9877), as the direct distance is only just over 100km (62 miles), taking around 90 minutes. However, do not rely on the ferry if you are on a tight schedule. There are just five departures per week in each direction, with no service on Friday or Sunday. In addition, the ferry regularly breaks down, or does not run in high seas or strong winds. Tickets are also cheaper for Egyptians, so the ferry can be fully booked when you try to buy one. Departures from Hurghadah are at 9am (except Wednesday at 4am), and from Sharm El Sheikh at 5pm (except Wednesday at 6pm).

## R

## RELIGION

Islam is the official religion, and roughly 90 percent of the population observe Islamic traditions and practices, mainly of the Sunni branch. Tourists wishing to visit any mosques should remove their shoes and avoid entering during Friday midday prayers, the holiest time of the week. Coptic Christians are the largest minority, who together with Jews and other Christian sects are free to worship at their own services in churches and synagogues. At St Catherine's Monastery, anyone dressed inappropriately will be asked to cover their bare legs.

## T

## TELEPHONES

The international code for Egypt is +20. The local code for Sharm El Sheikh and Dahab is 069. The code for Hurghadah, Al Qasir and Al Gunah is 065. Drop the 0 when calling internationally.

Most hotels offer direct dial services from your room, but these can be expensive. Better value are the private telephone shops in the towns.

**Mobile phones.** Bring your own phone, as the three major operators (Vodafone, Mobinil and Etisalat) have their own networks and agreements. If you intend using your mobile a lot or staying in Egypt for some time, consider buying a cheap local SIM card (with a local number) for better rates on internal and international calls.

## TIME ZONES

Egypt is two hours ahead of GMT, and there is summer daylight saving (making it one hour ahead of GMT) from late April to late September. Without any adjustments:

| New York | London | **Egypt** | Sydney | Auckland |
|----------|--------|-----------|--------|----------|
| 5am | 10am | **noon** | 7pm | 9pm |

## TIPPING

Even if you speak no Arabic, one word that you will definitely hear is *baksheesh*. This universal term when asking for a tip is used by everyone, whether they have done anything for you or not. Taxi drivers, ticket sellers and lift attendants all ask for *baksheesh,* even if their service has not been so great. These tips, relatively small in Western terms, are useful boosts to low family incomes.

## TOILETS

Most tourist sites are well equipped with good-quality toilets, maintained by an attendant who appreciates a small tip. Wandering around the towns there is no problem using the toilets of any restaurant, coffee shop, bar or hotel (but some larger hotels refuse to let non-residents inside). Carrying tissues or toilet paper is always a good idea.

| Where is the toilet? | **Fin el-hammam?** |
|----------------------|--------------------|

## TOURIST INFORMATION

The main Egyptian Tourist Authority office is at: Misr Travel Tower, Abassiya Square, Cairo, tel: 02 6841970, email: info@egypt.travel, www.egypt.travel. There are also many Egyptian Tourist Authority offices worldwide:

**UK:** Egyptian House, 170 Piccadilly, London W1V 9DD, tel: 020 7493 5283, email: info.uk@egypt.travel.

**US:** 630 Fifth Avenue, Suite 2305, New York, NY 10111, tel: (212) 332 2570, email: info.us@egypt.travel.

There are tourism offices at Youssef Afifi Street in Hurghadah (tel: 065-346 3034) and at the Hilton Taba Hotel in Taba (tel: 069-353 0010). At the individual hotels, most information and promotion is done by the private tour operators themselves, sometimes with desks, stands or information folders. Lots of tourist information can be obtained inside the free resort magazines and papers.

**V**

## VISAS AND ENTRY REQUIREMENTS

To enter Egypt, tourist and business visas are required for all nationalities except those from other Arab countries, and passports must be valid for a minimum of six months. Single-entry visas can be bought upon arrival by visitors of most nationalities. This is by far the easiest, quickest and cheapest way to obtain a visa – you don't even need a photograph. Single- and multiple-entry visas may also be obtained beforehand from an Egyptian Embassy or through a specialist visa company. Up to date information can be obtained from any tour operator, travel agency or visa specialist. Also check www.touregypt.net/visa.htm.

Passports will be required at your hotel upon arrival; staff will usually take a photocopy of the main details. If you are staying for longer than one month, visa extensions can be obtained at At Tur and Hurghadah. If you are staying for less than 15 days and you remain only inside the area between Sharm El Sheikh and Taba, the entry visa is free.

Most items of tourist baggage will be allowed into Egypt without any problem, but laptops and some digital equipment might be entered into your passport to ensure they leave when you do. There is a duty-free shop upon arrival at Hurghadah and Sharm El Sheikh international airports, with a personal allowance of one litre of spirits and two cartons of cigarettes.

## W

## WEBSITES AND INTERNET CAFÉS

Downtown areas have a few internet cafés, but they are sometimes hidden away on back streets or upstairs, so ask at the hotel. There are wifi connections at a few modern coffee shops and inside some hotels. Rates per hour vary greatly.

General tourist information websites include:
**www.egypt.travel** – official Egyptian Tourist Authority website
**www.touregypt.net** – a wealth of information provided by the Association of Egyptian Travel Businesses on the Internet
**www.cdws.travel** – Chamber of Diving and Water Sports for Egypt
**www.sis.gov.eg** – Egyptian State Information Service site, including live Egyptian TV and radio
**www.travellersinegypt.org** – fascinating articles about travel in Egypt from ancient times to the nineteenth century

Websites about the Sinai region:
**www.sinaiweekly.com** – local news and features
**www.allsinai.info** and **www.geographia.com/egypt/sinai/index.html** – information about the Sinai region
**www.sharmelsheikh.com** and **www.sharmguide.com** – general information about Sharm El Sheikh

**http://sharmwomen.com** – local site run by Sharm Women's Club
**www.dahab-info.com** – information about Dahab

Websites about the Hurghadah region:
**www.redsea.gov.eg** – official website of the Red Sea Governorate
**www.hurghadatour.com** – general information about Hurghadah
**www.elgouna.com** – official website for the Al Gunah resort

## WOMEN TRAVELLERS

Unwanted attention is the worst problem faced by most women visitors, especially those travelling on their own. Unfortunately, some
local Egyptian men see Western women as potentially easy sexual
partners. Very occasionally this will develop from lewd comments
to actual physical abuse. To avoid hassle, wear long, loose-fitting
clothing, and avoid non-tourist areas and poorly lit streets at night.
If you experience a problem, raise your voice in protest and make
nearby people aware – this will usually defuse the situation.

## Y

## YOUTH HOSTELS

There are Hostelling International hostels (www.hihostels.com,
www.egyptyha.com) in Sharm El Sheikh and Hurghadah (both
open 24 hours). These are not much different to a regular hotel,
but great value. As you can imagine, reservations are essential,
the maximum stay is 14 days and youth-hostel membership is
required.

**Hadaba Om Al Sayed** (opposite police station), Sharm El Sheikh,
tel: 069-366 0317, 069-366 2497, email: sharm.bookings@egypt
yha.com; 160 beds.

**Al Ghardaqah International**, 6km (4 miles) north of the city, close
to Al Gunah, tel: 065-350 0079, email: hurghada.bookings@egypt
yha.com; 200 beds.

## Recommended Hotels

From the Taba Hilton at the northern end of the Gulf of Aqaba down to Lahami Bay almost in the tropics, Egypt's Red Sea coast has hundreds of beach hotels and resorts to cater for every tourist's needs. The famous international chains provide top-class facilities in some of the most idyllic beachside locations.

Most inclusive flight and hotel packages use the string of resorts either side of Sharm El Sheikh and Hurghadah (Al Ghardaqah), but their locations on the outskirts make it more difficult for tourists to venture beyond the confines of their resort. When booking, try to get the name of the hotel and check its location, as there might be little in the way of local shops or restaurants on offer outside. The more distant resorts and hotels usually provide regular free shuttle buses into the town centres.

As a basic guide, the prices listed below are for a double room with private bathroom and air-conditioning, including breakfast and government taxes.

| | |
|---|---|
| $$$$$ | US$250 and above |
| $$$$ | US$125–250 |
| $$$ | US$80–125 |
| $$ | US$40–80 |
| $ | less than US$40 |

## SHARM EL SHEIKH

**Baron Resort $$$$$** *Ras Nasrani, tel: 069-367 0100, www. baron hotelsegypt.com*. Since it was one of the original resorts in Sharm El Sheikh, this large complex with 360 rooms has plenty of space and an enormous beachfront. The wonderful 'house' reef is reached by pontoon, and there are freshwater and seawater pools. If you can afford it, the two Royal suites even come with a butler.

**Beach Albatros $$$$** *Ras 'Om Sid, tel: 069-366 3922, www.pickalbatros.com*. One of the best-located hotels in Sharm, high on the clifftop overlooking Sharm Al Maya bay, giving fabulous views especially at sunset. A lift gives access directly onto the hotel beach.

**Club Magic Life Imperial $$$$** *Nabeq, tel: 069-371 0050, www. magiclife.com/en/home.html*. Very popular Andalusian-flavoured resort within extensive gardens and pools with plenty of activities, sports and entertainment. 521 rooms spread over 12 low-rise apartment buildings, about as far away from central Sharm as you can get. Choice of four restaurants including speciality Thai, Egyptian and fish.

**Eden Rock $$$** *Naama Bay Heights, tel: 069-360 2250, www.eden rockhotel.net*. A quieter hotel recently refurbished in an old Viennese boutique style with well-prepared food. No entertainment, but wonderful views across Naama Bay from the terraced pool.

**Four Seasons Sharm $$$$$** *Shark's Bay, tel: 069-360 3555, www. fourseasons.com/sharmelsheikh*. Wonderfully situated on a headland just 10 minutes' transfer to the airport. The five-star classification does not really do justice to the excellent service and facilities at this award-winning hotel. Secluded private beach, swimming pools, wellness, health and spa centres. With the possible exception of the Ritz-Carlton, this is as good as it gets.

**Hilton Waterfalls Resort $$$$$** *Ras 'Om Sid, tel: 069 366 3232, www.hilton.com/worldwideresorts*. Well established large resort of 401 rooms most of which overlook the sea. A series of terraces and pleasant pools drop down to the beach, featuring the pleasant Shish Bish – a relaxed outdoor sheesha and drinking terrace with great sea views.

**Iberotel Palace $$$$** *Sharm Al Maya Beach, tel: 069-366 1111, www.iberotel.com*. In a quiet area just 150m (164yds) from Old Sharm with its lively area of shops and restaurants. Many of the 243 rooms are located around the tiered pools which descend down to the beach. Full range of water sports.

**Jaz Mirabel Resort $$$$$** *Nabeq, tel: 069-371 0371, www.jaz resorts.com*. Situated within the spread of coastal resorts to the east of Sharm, but at the quieter Nabeq Protectorate end. Private beach with tennis courts, gym and spa centre. Pleasant terrace around the swimming pools.

**Jolie Ville Maritim Resort and Casino $$$$$** *Naama Bay, tel: 069-360 0100, www.jolieville-hotels.com.* Ideal central location in the heart of Naama Bay near lots of nightlife, bars and shops. Thai spa, wellness centre and top-class facilities throughout because this venue hosts many of the international conferences in Sharm El Sheikh.

**Marriott Beach Resort $$$$$** *Naama Bay, tel: 069-360 0190, www.marriott.com.* A large resort with over 500 rooms and a great location in Naama Bay. Facilities include indoor waterfalls and pools, and there are plenty of activity and restaurant choices, especially good Italian and sushi. The Marriott 'mountain' resort is set further back across Peace Road.

**Ritz-Carlton $$$$$** *Ras 'Om Sid, tel: 069-366 1919, www.ritzcarlton.com.* All 321 guest rooms at this resort are in low-rise apartments, each with a private terrace and the latest mod-cons. Facilities include several top-quality restaurants serving everything from Italian to Lebanese and Japanese cuisine, together with a cigar lounge, two big pools, waterfall, fitness centre and games room.

**Savoy Hotel $$$$$** *Soho Square, tel: 069-360 2500, www.savoy-sharm.com.* Part of a series of related resorts situated near to the airport along White Knight Beach. The 400 room Savoy is complimented by the 300 deluxe room Sierra and the more exclusive Royal Savoy, with its private wing and secluded facilities, Laid out in extensive lush gardens and pools that drop down to the large beach.

**Umbi Diving Village $$** *Shark's Bay, tel: 069-360 0942, www.sharksbay.com.* Established resort now completely renewed, yet still retaining its relaxing atmosphere. Choose a beach cabin, bamboo hut or room in the Bedouin Village perched on a small clifftop. Has a private beach with a beautiful coral reef and an excellent fish restaurant.

## ST CATHERINE'S

**Daniela $$** *St Catherine's Village, tel: 069-347 0379, www.daniela-hotels.com.* Spacious stone-built hotel in a spectacular location on high ground with 74 rooms split into small chalets or villas around the site, all with television. The ideal place to stay for a morning visit to the monastery or an attempt on Mount Sinai.

**Plaza \$\$\$** *St Catherine's Village, tel: 069-347 0289, www.catherine plaza.com.* This resort is set like an oasis in the mountainous desert with 168 rooms in villas, around a beautiful swimming pool. Restaurant, coffee shop and adventure centre for activities in this rugged area.

## DAHAB

**Blue Beach Club \$\$** *Asilah, tel: 069-364 0411, www.bluebeach club.com.* A small resort with 20 rooms around a swimming pool. Has a dive club and air-conditioned restaurant. Across the seafront is the beachside 'Furry Cup' bar, popular with the diving crowd in the evenings.

**Coral Coast \$\$** *Asilah, tel: 069-364 1195, 069-364 1690, www. embah.com.* Very quiet, relaxing locally run place with popular BSAC-affiliated dive centre and great open-air restaurant set alongside a beautiful beach. Located on the coast north of Dahab, from where desert safaris are expertly led into the tribal interior by Embah Safaris. 29 rooms in a two-floor building.

**Nesima \$\$\$** *Al Mashraba, tel: 069-364 0320, www.nesima-resort. com.* Good hotel and diving centre, inspired by traditional architecture, with lots of domes and a great swimming pool. Childcare is available. On the seafront, with great views and one of the best restaurants in Dahab.

## TABA HEIGHTS

**Hyatt Regency \$\$\$\$\$** *Taba Heights, tel: 069-358 0234, www.taba. regency.hyatt.com.* One of several large luxurious hotel chains in Taba Heights which share a golf course, marina and conference centre. Over 400 rooms, plus a wealth of facilities including casino, three pools, fitness centre and children's club all set within an 'Egyptian village' designed by architect Michael Graves.

## TABA

**Hilton Taba Resort and Nelson Village $$$$$** *tel: 069-353 0140, www.hilton.com/worldwideresorts.* Situated right at the border with Israel, this large 400-room hotel dominates the landscape, with fabulous views across the gulf to Jordan and Saudi Arabia. Full choice of water sports, restaurants and bars, including Nelson's bar right on the beach.

## RAS SUDR

**Moon Beach Retreat $$** *tel: 010-581 0088.* The perfect location for water-sports adrenalin junkies, with continual windy conditions to test any keen wind- or kitesurfer. Ideal for both beginners and pros, with equipment to rent or buy, but there's not much else in the local area, apart from yoga and massage.

## SUEZ

**Red Sea $$$** *13 Al Riad Street, Port Tewfik, tel: 062-319 0190.* This 80-room hotel is in a quiet garden suburb right beside the canal. The best place to stay in the Suez area within the quiet Port Tewfik suburb. Fabulous views from the sixth-floor restaurant when the ships are in convoy through the canal, but it's a pity the food is not better.

## AL GUNAH

**Captain's Inn $$$** *Abu Tig Marina, tel: 065-358 0170, www.el gouna.com.* A small, stylish boutique guest house with 48 rooms overlooking the marina. Centrally located near the shopping outlets, restaurants and nightlife at Abu Tig Marina, with live music every Monday evening. Residents can use the pools at the nearby Ocean View.

**Sheraton Miramar Resort $$$$$** *tel: 065-354 5606, www.sheraton. com/elgouna.* This 338-room hotel offers world-class architecture by American architect Michael Graves, who was inspired by the work of the late Egyptian architect Hassan Fathy. Painted in muted primary colours and built in a simple low-rise style, the hotel is surrounded by turquoise lagoons with small quiet beaches and water-sport centres.

**Steigenberger Golf Resort $$$$$** *tel: 065-358 0140, www.steigen berger.com.* This luxurious golf resort, designed by Michael Graves, won a prestigious award from the American Institute for Architects. Surrounded by Al Gunah's blue lagoons and 18-hole USPGA championship golf course, it caters for both golfers and upmarket holidaymakers. Excellent food in its three restaurants with impeccable service.

## HURGADAH (AL GHARDAQAH)

**Beirut $$$** *Corniche Street, Sakala, tel: 065-354 8906, www.beirut hotels-eg.com.* In a fabulous location on the coast road near Ad-Dahar, with a pool and terrace. It's relatively small at 132 rooms, and there aren't many facilities or shops within the immediate vicinity.

**Golden Sun $** *Al Arosa Square, Sheraton Street, downtown Sakala, tel: 065-344 4403, tel: 012-362 5102, email: goldenkhalid@hot mail.com.* Good-value rooms with TVs, air-conditioning and fridges. Good location near to many bars, shops and restaurants.

**Golf $** *Sheraton Road, Sakala (facing Commercial Centre), tel: 065-344 2828.* Good-value hotel in a great central location, even though rooms on the front can be a bit noisy, due to the main road. Lively rooftop pool and terrace when hotel full.

**Iberotel Makadi Beach $$$$$**, *Makadi Bay, tel: 069 359 0000, www.iberotel.com.* One of several resorts, including a golf club that makes up 'Madinet Makadi' 35kms south of Hurgadah. The hotel's 313 rooms are situated in extensive parkland and beach area. Safe 'house reef' for beginner divers, ideal for families with plenty activities, including waterpark and waterslides. Partakes in the 'dine around' programme of Makadi Bay.

**Intercontinental Resort and Casino $$$$$** *Village Road, tel: 065-346 5100, www.ichotelsgroup.com.* One of the large coastal resorts to the south of Hurgadah, not far from the airport. Recently renovated with a mixture of Islamic, Greek and ancient Egyptian architecture. There are five international-cuisine restaurants, plus fitness and massage centres.

**Roma $$$** *Hadaba Road, Sakala, tel: 065-344 8141.* Popular with tour groups, but with 139 rooms over five floors it can seem crowded. There's a pool on the second floor and a nightclub downstairs. Private beach area with pool and restaurant across the road.

**Safir Hotel $$$$** *End of Sheraton Road, tel: 065-344 2901, www. safirhotels.com.* Fabulous location on a headland with a pool and dive club and probably the best beach in Hurgadah, yet only 10 minutes from the airport. 141 rooms, five restaurants, dive centre, private marina and pier for fishing.

**Sahl Hashish Oberoi $$$$$** *On the Sahl Hashish coast, 25 minutes' drive south of central Hurgadah, tel: 065-344 0777, www. oberoihotels.com.* The most exclusive all-suite luxury hotel on this coast, set in 19 hectares (48 acres) of palm-filled grounds, with 850m (930yds) of private sandy beach. This environmentally friendly resort is sumptuous, with domed pavilions and traditionally inspired contemporary Arabic architecture.

**Sea Garden $$$** *Sakala, between Al Arosa Square and the sea, tel: 065-344 7492, www.seagarden.com.eg.* In the heart of Sakala between Al Arosa Square and the Ministry of Sound beach club. Uninspiring to look at from outside, but comfortable rooms and good swimming pool. Popular with small groups passing through on a tour of Egypt, rather than people staying for a week or two.

**Sea View $** *Corniche Street, Ad Dahar, tel: 065-354 5959, www.sea viewhotel.com.eg.* Family-owned hotel run to high standards by a former official antiquities guide from Luxor (Al Uqsur). The swimming pool is within the indoor restaurant. Excellent value for such a prime seafront location, but some of the lower-floor rooms at the front can be noisy due to traffic.

**Shedwan Garden $$$** *Corniche Road, Ad Dahar, tel: 065-355 5052, www.redseahotels.com.* Large older-style complex with a vast expanse of beach and a long sandbar stretching into the sea. Several pools, lots of children's and sporting activities with an old-fashioned holiday camp atmosphere.

**Triton Empire $$** *Hospital and Sayed Korrayem Street, Ad Dahar, tel: 065-354 9200, www.threecorners.com.* Good-value hotel set in two buildings within the Ad Dahar suburb about 500m (550yds) from the sea, but with access to a beach club for guests. Two swimming pools at the hotel and two at the beach. Great location for lively nightlife and shops.

**Zak Royal Wings $$** *Sheraton Road, middle of new Sakala, tel: 065-344 6012.* Older-style hotel, but in a great position near the beach, shops and many family restaurants. All 41 rooms have balconies overlooking the large pool, great for families.

## ABU SOMA

**Intercontinental Resort $$$$$** *tel: 065-326 0700, www.ichotels group.com.* A large resort with 445 rooms in an idyllic quiet location 45km (28 miles) south of Hurgadah. Spacious beach bordering two sweeping bays protected by palm trees. Restaurants specialising in Italian, Lebanese and Greek cuisine.

## SAFAJAH

**Al Remal $$** *In front of Safajah Port, tel: 065-325 7316, www.remal hotel.com.* Ideally situated for catching a ferry from the port, but in quite a busy area with port traffic. 100 rooms, all with sea views. Provides a free shuttle bus to its large private beach, five minutes away.

**Nemo Dive Club and Hotel $$** *Maglis Madina, Corniche Street, tel: 065-325 6777, 010-364 8708, www.nemodive.com.* A new 30-room Belgian/Dutch-managed hotel 3km (2 miles) north of the main centre, specialising in catering for divers keen to explore the area and affiliated to most diving organisations. Great value as it is all-inclusive. Wonderful views from the rooftop restaurant and bar where the day's dives are discussed.

## AL QASIR

**El-Quseir Hotel $** *Corniche, tel: 065-333 2301.* There are just six rooms in this 19th-century converted Ottoman merchant's house overlooking the sea. Unique along the entire coastline, but there are few concessions to the 21st century, so shared bathrooms and no air-conditioning. A great opportunity to experience a wonderfully restored and atmospheric building.

**Mövenpick Resort $$$$$** *Sirena Beach, Al Qadim Bay, tel: 065-333 2100, www.moevenpick-quseir.com.* Beautifully designed resort with 250 domed rooms built and decorated in traditional style. Excellent service and facilities. Highly recommended if you want a few days of peace and quiet or to dive from the Subex Red Sea diving centre. Located at the old entrance to the ancient Myos Hormos port.

## MARSA SHAGRA

**Red Sea Diving Safari $$$** *Marsa Shagra, 20km (12 miles) north of Marsa' Alam, tel: 02-3337 1833, 02-3337 9942, fax: 02-3749 4219, www.redsea-divingsafari.com.* For those wanting to get away from the Hurghada sprawl, this is ideal. A great eco-lodge where unlimited 'house' reef dives are included in the price. Owner Hossam Helmi is a committed environmentalist who deliberately keeps the place small to limit environmental impact.

## LAHAMI BAY

**Lahami Bay Beach Resort $$$$$** *115km (71 miles) south of Marsa' Alam, tel: 012-317 3344, 019-510 0354, fax: 012-316 8410, www.lahamibay.com.* Luxury and seclusion at the furthest resort south along the coast. This series of white colonial-style villas set around a quiet lagoon is a great place to relax. Bars, pools, restaurants, squash court, volleyball and gym. The resort's dive centre offers safe 'house' reef dives, as well as daily boat dives to a variety of offshore reefs.

# INDEX

**Berlitz** pocket guide

# Egypt
# Red Sea Coast

**Second Edition 2012**

Written by Chris Bradley
Edited by Tony Halliday
Series Editor: Tom Stainer

Photography credits
All pictures by Chris Bradley except: akg-images 19, 22; Arnaud/hemis.fr/Egyptian Tourist Authority 13, 98; Glynn Genin/APA 4B, 83, 94, 108; iStockphoto 3TL, 5BR, 5TL, 8, 24, 26, 31, 42, 80, 84, 88; Axel Krause 2T; Little Budha Bar 5TR, 93; Andy Pawson/ Fotoseeker 4R, 33, 67, 87; St Catherine's Monastery 20, 36; SUNRISE Tirana Aqua Park Pool 97; Ming Tang-Evans/APA 4–5; Topfoto 16.

Cover picture: 4Corners Images

Every effort has been made to provide accurate information in this publication, but changes are inevitable. The publisher cannot be responsible for any resulting loss, inconvenience or injury.

**Contact us**

At Berlitz we strive to keep our guides as accurate and up to date as possible, but if you find anything that has changed, or if you have any suggestions on ways to improve this guide, then we would be delighted to hear from you.

Berlitz Publishing, PO Box 7910, London SE1 1WE, England.
email: berlitz@apaguide.co.uk
www.berlitzpublishing.com